Editor-in-Chief: Barrie Pitt
Editor: David Mason
Art Director: Sarah Kingham
Picture Editor: Robert Hunt
Designer: David A Evans
Cover: Denis Piper
Special Drawings: John Weal
Photographic Research: Nan Shuttleworth

Photographs for this book were specially selected from the author's private collection and on pages 20 and 57 from Paul Popper Ltd

First Printing: February, 1971

Printed in the United States of America

Ballantine Books, Inc.
101 Fifth Avenue, New York, N.Y.

An Intext Publisher

Contents

The devil's broomstick

Introduction by Barrie Pitt

No aircraft enthusiast will need to be told that the author of Rocket Fighter is an acknowledged authority; William Green's reputation in his field is international. The mass of works of which he is the author, and those innumerable others in the production of which his collaboration and advice have proved indispensable, are universally conceded to be the final court of appeal in the settlement of any question of doubt concerning the history of aviation. The reader is in the best possible hands.

In the story of powered flight the place of the manned rocket fighter is highly unusual. In that story there have been many more or less radical departures from conventional thinking since the quietly epoch-making day at Kitty Hawk. For the most part they have in time been adopted, developed and are still with us, or, if badly mistaken, were quickly dropped. The rocket fighter's hectic history, begun and finished in scarcely more than a decade, is hard to place in either category.

On the face of it a machine offering a speed advantage of possibly 300mph (an Me 163B V18 Komet clocked 702mph on 6th July 1944), a fantastic rate of climb and a ceiling to top any piston engined aircraft should have given its possessor an unbeatable advantage. The glorious promise was doomed to be broken. To set against those glowing recommendations are very serious disadvantages. The first and, it would be thought, obviously fatal flaw is the extremely short endurance inherent in a propulsion system which, even in those early days, drank its fuel in units of pounds per second. Six or seven minutes – at the most – of combat time are hardly enough, and even superior speed carries its own hidden penalty underlining that damning factor: it takes that much longer to turn back after making a pass.

In practice problems also arose with the Komet because no armament suiting the performance of the aircraft had been developed. When existing cannon were mounted their effective range and accuracy – to say nothing of the reflexes of the pilot – were inadequate to deal with the new order of speed; the target might be at optimum distance for a second or less. A multitude of similar difficulties were encountered, and added to them was the unavoidable and, for the pilot, quite disturbing knowledge that he was flying a tank of hideously unstable high explosive.

At root the setbacks, horrifying accidents and ultimate failure of the rocket fighter programmes at that moment in time were due to the fact that the aircraft from which so much was expected were airborne assemblies of question marks. A welter of new disciplines was involved: the handling and storage of corrosive, volatile and unstable liquids in variable conditions, the abstruse math of high temperature gas flow in continuous burning, cryogenics, the geometry of combustion chambers and fuel nozzles, the metallurgy to cope with the range and variation of temperatures and pressures encountered, near sound speed aerodynamics, and many more.

Even these might have been mastered. In the USSR however, after very promising beginnings (the first genuine manned rocket powered interceptor in the world, the Russian BI, flew on 15th May 1942, predating the Germans' first by some fifteen months; it 'flew like the devil's broomstick,' said a pilot), the programme died of neglect and politics. In Germany it came to flower when the surviving industrial capability of the Reich – and the necessary specialists – were spread too thin to give it the sort of priority which alone could have made it viable; and in the end it killed more of its own pilots than Allied ones. In Japan it was nipped in the bud by unconditional surrender. In Britain, a sad story . . . In the USA much worthwhile and exciting work was done but the technical problems finally seemed just too great, and the number of accidents was effective in cooling the required ardour.

So it would seem that in large part it was the time and resources question which prevented at least one programme from achieving its end. And yet, had the rocket fighter been allowed a few more years of war to develop into a reliable weapon, would it have been decisive or even particularly significant? The day of the jet aircraft, the effective ground-to-air and air-to-air rocket missiles, and of the ICBM, was already dawning, and in one way or another the rocket fighter would surely have found itself outclassed or its services no longer required. Its rapid demise on the cessation of hostilities shows that this point has been generally agreed.

However, in its brief lifetime, scarcely long enough to allow it to take the first step on to the stage of history, it attracted to itself some of the best brains and most courageous of men. Those pilots, riding tails of fire, were pointing directly to the Space Age.

Birth of a concept

Eight P-51 Mustangs of the AAF's 359th Fighter Group, led by the Group's Commanding Officer, Colonel Avelin P Tacon Jr, cruised on a southerly heading in the thin clear air some 25,000 feet above Merseburg, a few miles west of Leipzig. It was 28th July 1944, and flying from their Norfolk base of East Wretham, the Mustangs were providing close escort for 45th Bombardment Wing B-17 Fortresses, which, having completed their strike, were now droning sedately homeward, their nearest combat box about 1,000 yards to starboard of Colonel Tacon's octet of 'little friends'. Suddenly, one of the P-51 pilots called in two contrails at six o'clock high – extraordinarily thick white vapour tracks as dense as cumulus cloud and three-quarters of a mile in length scarring the sky some five miles aft and 5,000 feet above the AAF elements. Colonel Tacon hastily turned his P-51s through 180 degrees to place the small fighter force between his charges and a menacing new enemy weapon; it was the most spectacular interceptor that was to be brought to combat status by any nation in the Second World War – the Messerschmitt Me 163B Komet.

This rocket-driven warplane, the existence of which had been known to Allied intelligence for more than a year, promised to pose near-insuperable problems for the AAF's long-range fighters, whose task was the protection of the immense formations of 8th and 15th Air Force day bombers engaged in cutting the industrial heart from Germany's Third Reich. The Komet's début on the aerial battlefield had been awaited by AAF and RAF alike with something approaching trepidation. Now this radical airplane had actually appeared in service, climbing, as one 359th Group pilot succinctly commented, 'like a bat out of hell', far above the effective combat ceilings of the bombers and their escorting fighters.

Had the Allies' worst fears been realised? It certainly appeared so when the crews of B-17s which provided the Komet with some of its first potential victims reported that the rocket-propelled Messerschmitt travelled too fast to be tracked by their turrets or free guns. There was understandable alarm at the Headquarters of the 8th Air Force in High Wycombe and at USSTAF Headquarters at Bushey Park. If the Luftwaffe could put up enough of these revolutionary little airplanes the continuation of the daylight offensive against major German industrial targets could well become too hazardous.

On the day following this first encounter with the Komet, the rocket-driven interceptor again put in an appearance in the vicinity of Merseburg. Captain Arthur J Jeffrey of the P-38J Lightning-equipped 479th Fighter Group, escorting a straggling 100th Bombardment Group B-17 at about 11,000 feet above Wesermünde, and believing that he had knocked down an Me 163B with a deflection shot from some 300 yards, was awarded a 'kill', though undeservedly as time was to prove. The AAF believed that it had drawn first blood in what could well be the opening paragraph of a new chapter in the story of aerial warfare in German skies, but the advent of this unorthodox menace to the strategic bombing programme was nonetheless worrying. Unbeknown to the Allies, however, the Komet was affording the Luftwaffe far more worries than would have resulted from combat attrition, and had come within an ace of being stillborn.

While the application of the liquid-propellant rocket motor to a combat aircraft had not been purely a result of wartime expediency, there could be no doubt that the exigencies of war had dictated its premature realisation. Nor was there any doubt that, at the time it was first encountered over Merseburg, the rocket-propelled warplane was the most *dramatic* development in interceptor fighter evolution since the first synchronised machine gun had chattered from a Fokker E I during the First World War, but events were to prove it less efficacious.

The problems inherent in the design of an effective rocket-propelled interceptor were by no means simple of solution, as Soviet aircraft designers in that summer of 1944 were already painfully aware, and as US aircraft designers also were rapidly learning. Yet, despite a dauntingly voracious appetite for highly volatile fuels with lethal propensities in consequence, the liquid-fuel rocket motor was endowed with unique features, and exercised a magnetic attraction for a handful of the more audacious visionaries in the ranks of aircraft designers – an attraction which was to be maintained for something like a decade after the Luftwaffe first committed rocket-driven fighters to battle.

Fortuitously, the concept of the target-defence interceptor driven by a liquid-propellant rocket motor found adherents in both Germany and the Soviet Union at about the same time. Both countries had conducted experiments with solid- and liquid-fuel rockets from the mid 1920s, though neither had given serious consideration to their potential as a means of aircraft propulsion until the mid 1930s. However, the awakening of interest in the rocket as a primary source of power for manned military aircraft had been predated a number of years by several rocket-driven airplanes of less serious intent, the motivation behind those developed in Germany, at least, had been more a desire for publicity on the part of their promoters than a wish to further knowledge. The spectacular had overshadowed the significant, and thus rocket propulsion was widely considered by the serious-minded as no more than a *divertissement* for the man in the street, possessing all the characteristics of a highly dangerous stunt and none of those of a realistic means of propelling an aircraft.

Finance for the early experiments in Germany was largely provided by the automobile magnate Fritz von Opel. His reasons for subsidising rocket propulsion trials were anything but altruistic. Apart from embodying an element of risk, which he found a diverting challenge, Opel saw the rocket as a spectacular means of publicising his company, and this publicity was to be the sole tangible result of the somewhat extraordinary series of experiments conducted under the direction of Max Valier, a leading light in the Verein für Raumschiffahrt (VFR), or Society for Space Navigation. The Society had been founded in Breslau in June 1927 as a direct result of a mathematical treatise entitled *The Rocket into Interplanetary Space* by Professor Hermann Oberth.

On the surface it seemed that the title of the organisation was a misnomer. One of the primary aims of the VFR was the enlistment of popular support for experiments in rocketry; the removal of rocket propulsion from the abstraction of technical theses and the demonstration of its power to the ordinary man.

Oberth's treatise stressed the superiority of the liquid- to the solid-propellant rocket, but the use of liquid propellants for rockets was still largely theoretical. They had barely seen application, and what tests had been conducted were largely confined to the work of Robert H. Goddard of Clark University in Worcester, Massachusetts, which had culminated on 16th March 1926 in the launching of a small rocket driven by liquid oxygen and gasoline. To the band of enthusiastic purists working at the so-called Raketenflugplatz, or Rocket Airfield, of the VFR on an abandoned ammunition dump at Reinickendorf, Berlin, the solid (powder) rocket was primitive and possessed virtually no significance insofar as their research was concerned. Max Valier, however, was shrewd enough to perceive that widespread popular support, and with it the funds with which to finance serious research, could only be obtained by spectacle; that spectacle could only be offered to the public by recourse to the crude solid-fuel rocket, as liquid-propellant rockets had barely begun their development cycle. Thus, although Valier shared Oberth's view that only the liquid-fuel rocket had a serious future as a means of propulsion, he put forward ideas for propelling aircraft, cars and other vehicles by means of batteries of powder rockets, and these ideas immediately captured Opel's imagination.

With the aid of Alexander Sander, a pyrotechnist at Wesermünde, Valier

One of the hair-raising flights of the Opel-Sander Rak. 1

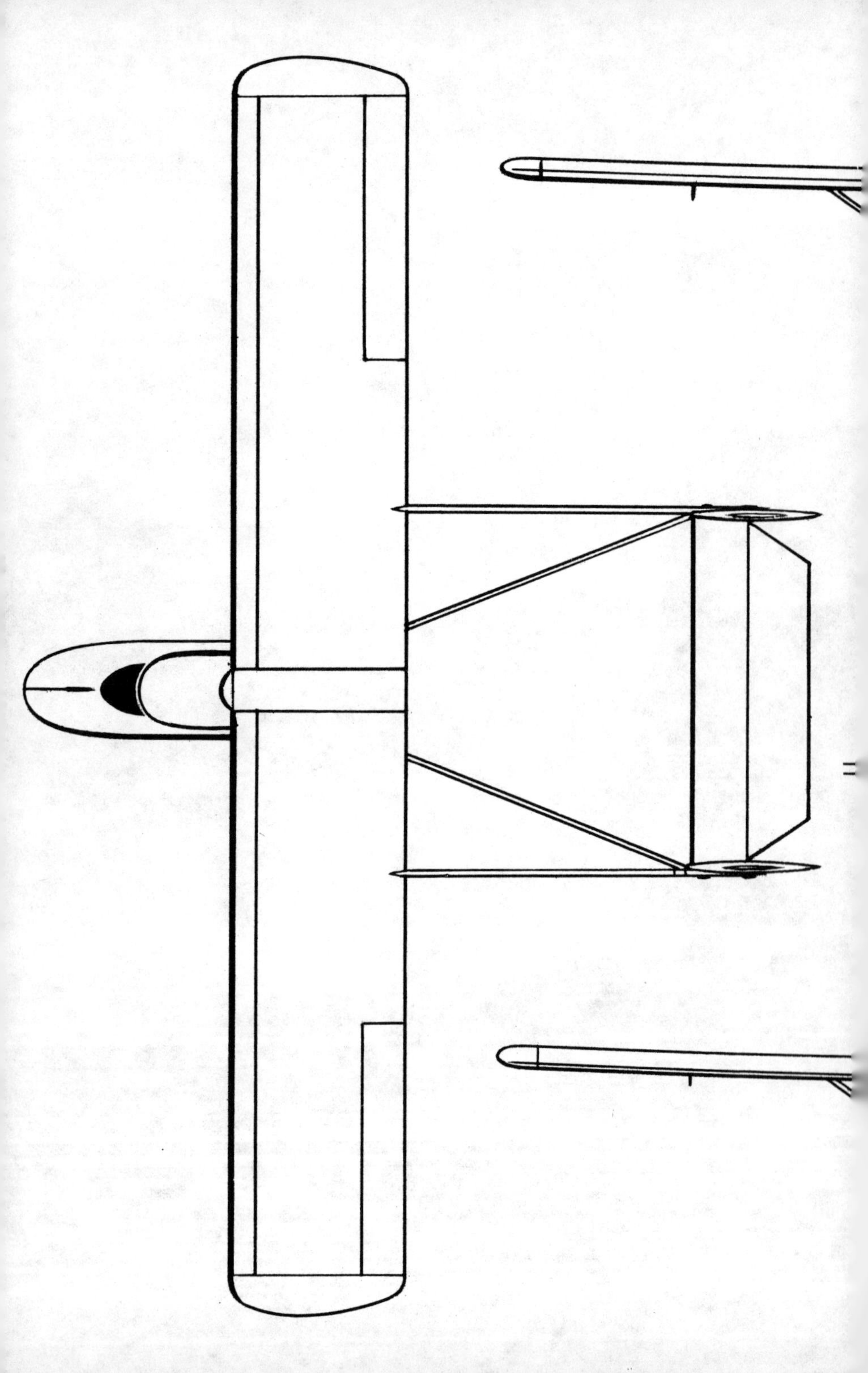

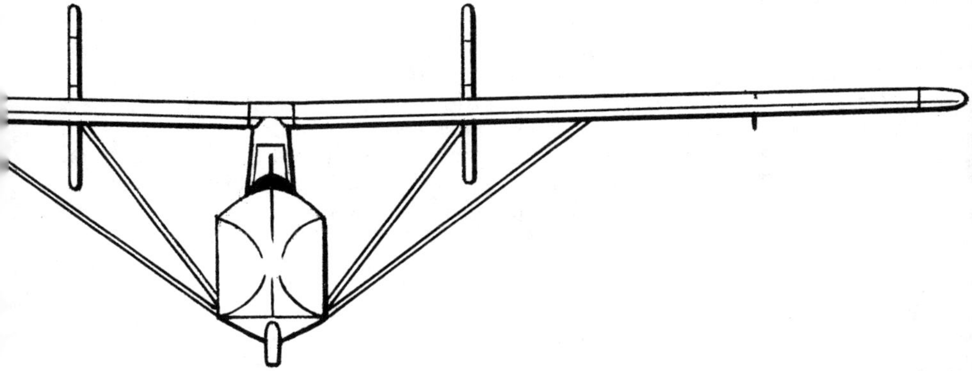

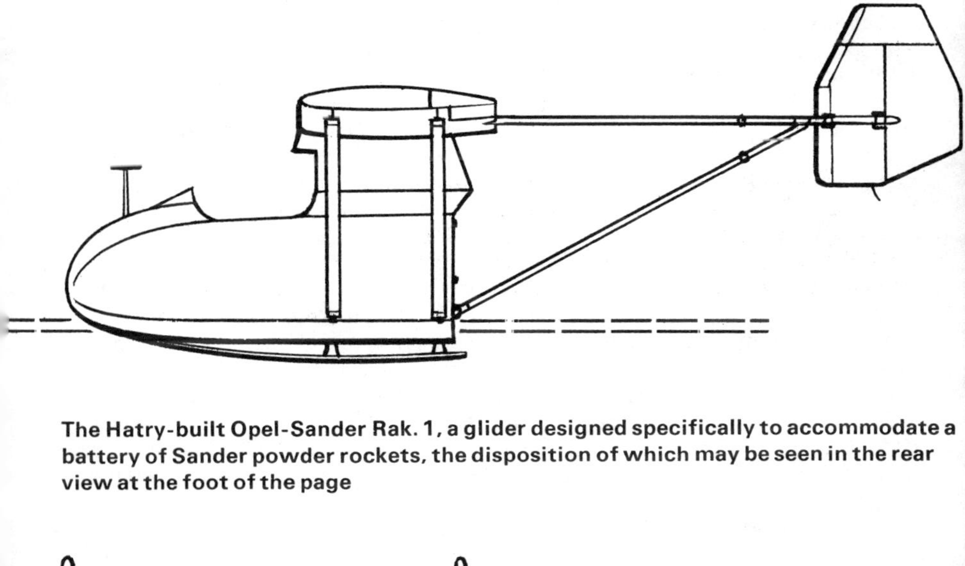

The Hatry-built Opel-Sander Rak. 1, a glider designed specifically to accommodate a battery of Sander powder rockets, the disposition of which may be seen in the rear view at the foot of the page

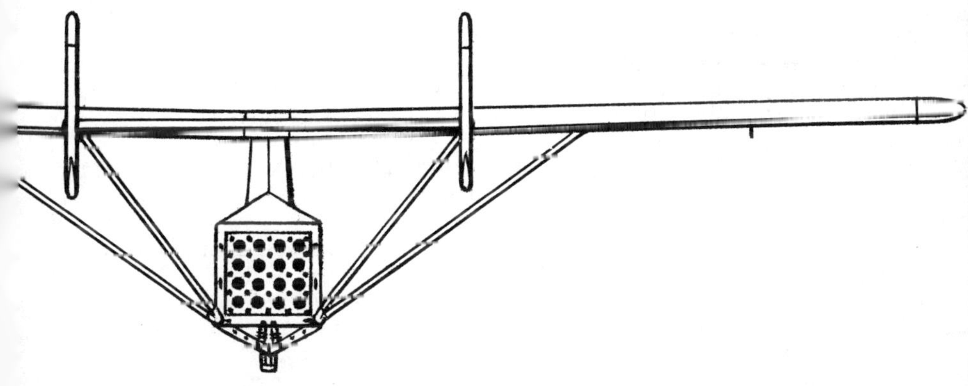

evolved a propulsion system combining high-thrust, fast-burning powder rockets for initial acceleration with lower-thrust, slower-burning rockets to sustain velocity. With Fritz von Opel's financial support, tests with the rocket propulsion of both aircraft and cars began almost simultaneously in 1928. An engineer named Hatry was commissioned to design and build a rocket-propelled glider which was to be known as the Opel-Sander Rak. 1; work began in the Opel factory on a rocket-driven automobile, the Opel Rak. 2, and Opel approached Alexander M Lippisch, a young designer working at the Rhön-Rossitten-Gesellschaft (RRG), who had already displayed a penchant for the unorthodox in airplane configuration, with the proposal that he, too, design a glider for rocket power.

Max Valier and Alexander Sander also succeeded in arousing enthusiasm for rocket propulsion in a twenty-seven-year-old aircraft designer, Gottlob 'Espe' Espenlaub, whose small factory at Wuppertal, near Düsseldorf, built light wooden sports aircraft and gliders when orders for them were forthcoming, and household furniture when they were not. Espenlaub agreed to modify an EA 1 glider of his own design for tests with the Sander powder rockets as the Espenlaub-Valier Rak. 3. Furthermore, he enlisted the aid of a Swiss engineer, A Sohldenhoff, to design and construct a tailless aircraft, the E 15, specifically for rocket propulsion.

Test runs with the Rak. 2 rocket-driven car were performed by Opel himself at Rüsselsheim during the spring of 1928, and after several disappointing trials he succeeded in clocking a speed of 137 mph on 23rd May during a demonstration run over the Avus in Berlin, a total of twenty-four rockets being ignited in relays. Less than three weeks later, on 11th June, Fritz Stamer effected the first rocket-propelled flight in Lippisch's glider, travelling a distance of 4,000 feet in seventy seconds.

The glider had been dubbed Ente, or Duck, as a result of its tail-first configuration which followed closely that of the similarly-named Focke-Wulf F 19 in which Georg Wulf had lost his life during the previous year. Vertical surfaces were attached to the wing which was braced above the aft end of the fuselage, and this housed the pilot and a bank of Sander rockets. It carried horizontal surfaces above its fore end. The brief flight was, at best, a qualified success, Stamer having found the Ente to be barely controllable during its brief sortie from the ground under rocket power. Two further flight tests were attempted, the second of which terminated abruptly when one of the extremely temperamental powder rockets exploded, and Lippisch, as yet by no means a convert to the ranks of the rocket propulsion enthusiasts, reverted to more orthodox means of propulsion, although fate was to decree reacquaintance with the rocket power plant a few years later.

Early in 1929, 'Espe' Espenlaub began testing the Rak. 3 at Düsseldorf, in which two staggered and vertically-disposed rockets were mounted above the wing, aft of the cockpit. The only concessions to the extremely high temperatures of the gases ejected by the rockets were a small steel plate beneath and aft of the rockets them selves, and the sheathing with light metal of a portion of the vertical stabilizer bathed by the exhaust gases. The initial arrangement of the rockets on the airplane centreline quickly gave place to a side-by-side arrangement, and for crude measurements of the thrust exerted by the rockets, a number of ground runs were made with the Rak.3 tethered by elastic cables. Only one or two short hops had been attempted before the tail caught fire, and Espenlaub, tacitly admitting that the EA 1 did not possess the most desirable configuration for such experiments, shelved the entire programme pending availability of the specially-designed E 15.

Espenlaub (with foot on fuselage) and Sander (in cap) with the Rak. 3

Meanwhile, the Opel-Sander Rak.1 had been finally completed by Hatry. This was a braced monoplane with a high-mounted wing and an abbreviated nacelle to accommodate the pilot and a bank of sixteen rockets, with splayed lattice-type booms raising the tail surfaces clear of the rocket exhaust. The rockets afforded a total thrust of some 900 pounds, the intention being to ignite these in relays with the Rak.1 accelerating along a raised track believed to be of sufficient length for flying speed to be attained. On 30th September 1929, the Rak.1 was readied at Frankfurt-Rebstock for its first flight. Fritz von Opel sat at the controls, and after two mis-starts, when the failure of individual rockets prevented flying speed being attained, he succeeded in lifting the aircraft from the track and remained airborne for a distance of nearly 5,000 feet, attaining a maximum velocity of ninety-five mph.

This flight aroused much excitement, and further tests were attempted using more powerful rockets, but during one of these the Rak.1 landed heavily and sustained extensive damage. Opel himself suffered only superficial injuries, but having sustained a number of disappointments as a result of trials with his rocket-driven car, knowing the unstable nature of Sander's powder rockets, and believing that he had extracted as much publicity as was likely to result from these spectacular demonstrations, he withdrew further financial support from the VFR.

Espenlaub's E 15 tailless aircraft had been completed during the course of 1929, and while it accommodated its pilot in an underslung nacelle as did the Ente and the Rak.1, its rockets were mounted on the trailing edge of the wing centre section, and a more conventional means of taking off was afforded by a simple reverse-tricycle undercarriage. Elementary caution

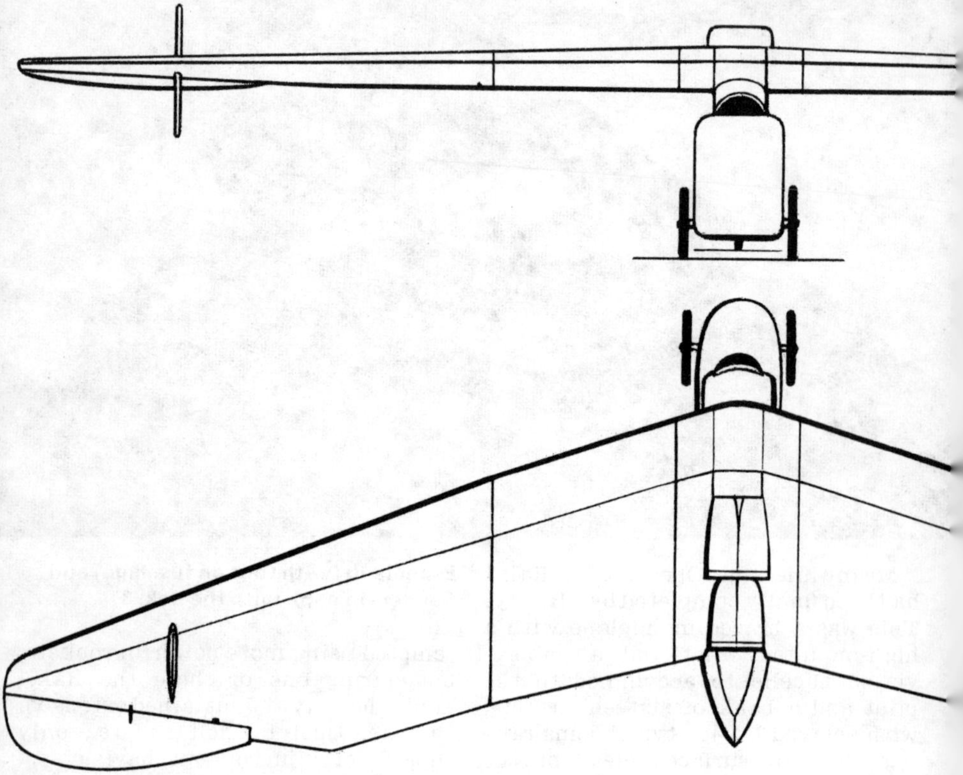

The Espenlaub E 15 tailless monoplane. The E 15 was fitted with two banks of Sander powder rockets above the centre section of its wing, and after preliminary tests with a piston engine it flew several times under rocket power

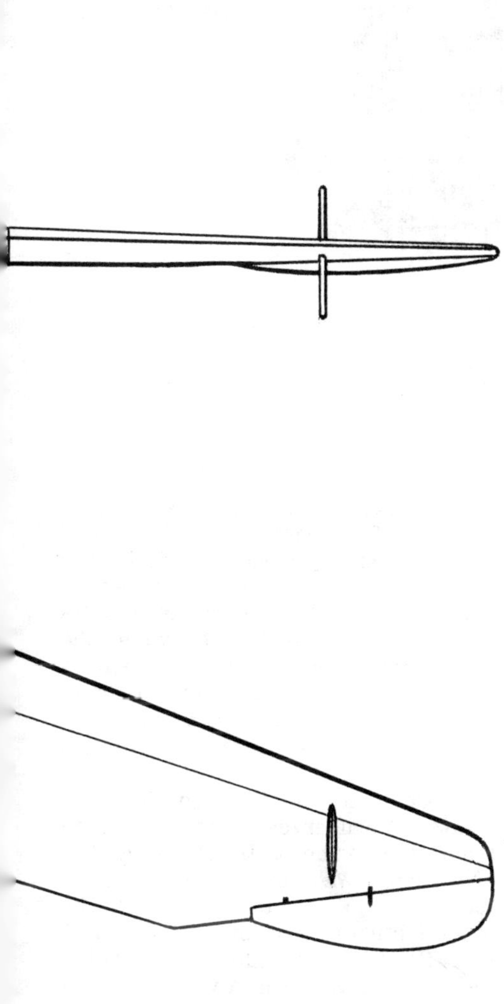

dictated a series of flight tests with a 20hp Daimler engine in order to evaluate handling characteristics, and once these had been established, the piston engine was removed and powder rockets installed under Sander's supervision. Those for initial acceleration and take-off each offered about 180 pounds of thrust, and those intended to sustain speed once the E 15 had left the ground each offered approximately twenty pounds.

After completing a series of ground trials, Espenlaub flew the E 15 under rocket power for the first time on 4th May 1930 at Bremerhaven. Several other tests were performed without any positive results, and during one of these Espenlaub inadvertently ignited in flight one of the more powerful rockets that had malfunctioned during the actual take-off. The aircraft immediately adopted a nose-down attitude from which, owing to the low altitude, there was no possibility of recovering, though Espenlaub survived the crash to join the growing ranks of those disenchanted with this radical method of propelling aircraft.

Thus, the beginning of the 1930s saw the end of the solid-propellant rocket as a primary power source for aircraft. Abroad, these rocket-driven aircraft, coupling unorthodox propulsion with equally unorthodox configurations, were seen as degenerate expressions of the designer's art, and it is true that they had contributed little of significance to power plant development. They had however fulfilled their primary purpose – the raising of money for the more serious experimentation with liquid-propellant rocket motors with which tangible progress was at last being made. Max Valier himself survived Espenlaub's final rocket-propelled flight by only a few days, meeting a pioneer's death on 17th May 1930 at the Heylandt-Worke at Bretz, near Berlin, when a liquid-propellant rocket motor on which he was working exploded.

'To be burned before reading'

The abandoning of this spectacular series of experiments with rocket-driven aircraft and cars, which had been accompanied by extensive coverage in the German popular press, was understandably followed by an immediate decline in public interest in rocketry, and the continuation of work on liquid-fuel rocket motors at the Reinickendorf Raketenflugplatz was rendered progressively more difficult by a chronic shortage of funds. The experiments had not gone entirely unnoticed by the German Army Weapons Department (Heereswaffenamt), however, and some interest in the potentialities of rocket-propulsion for military purposes was being evinced by Dr (later General) Becker, head of the Department's Ballistics and Munitions Branch. Thus, following the submission of a report on the subject to the Reichswehr, it had been decided, late in 1929, that some research should be undertaken into rocketry on an official but strictly clandestine basis.

The first objective at this stage was the development of an inexpensive weapon capable of launching a pattern of warhead - carrying solid-fuel rockets against targets within a range of three to five miles. The second objective was the design and construction of a simple liquid-fuel rocket for study and experimentation. Some financial support was secretly provided for various individuals and groups that appeared to be following promising lines in the development of rocket motors, but no positive results had been achieved by 1932 when the Department decided to establish its own experimental centre in a clearing in the Brandenburg pinewoods at Kummersdorf, about seventeen miles south of Berlin.

A Captain (later Major-General) Walter Dornberger, who had been appointed to the Ballistics Council of the Army Weapons Department in 1930, was placed in charge of the establishment, and one of his first recruits at Kummersdorf was a youthful Wernher von Braun who had been working at the Reinickendorf Raketenflugplatz. He was soon joined by Walter Riedel, a former colleague of Max Valier from the Heylandt-Werke. Around this nucleus, Dornberger built up a small but enthusiastic team which began work on a liquid-propellant motor, the A 1, intended to provide a thrust of 650 pounds, but the development of this rocket was still in its early stages when, in 1933, Hitler and the National Socialist Party assumed the leadership of Germany. The records of the VFR were pre-empted, and all rocket development became so highly classified that those involved commented cynically that all documents might as well be stamped 'To be burned before reading!'

Work at Kummersdorf was, at this time, ostensibly directed solely towards developing the liquid-fuel rocket motor as a potential power plant for a missile, although the fertile imagination of Wernher von Braun already forsaw a variety of other possible applications for the rocket, including its use as a means of assisting heavily-laden airplanes to leave the ground, and as a power plant for high-speed, fast-climbing interceptor fighters. Concurrently and quite independently of Dornberger's group at Kummersdorf, a young engineer named Hellmuth Walter, working at the Germania-Werft, Kiel, was struggling with the problems posed by a liquid-propellant rocket motor, but his primary purpose was the perfection of a wakeless marine torpedo propulsion unit. Whereas the Kummersdorf motor used methyl alcohol and liquid oxygen, Walter's motor used hydrogen peroxide, the chief product of the decomposition of which was superheated steam which rapidly condensed in water and thus left no wake.

Initially, Walter had experienced considerable difficulty in obtaining hydrogen peroxide of sufficient concentration for his purpose, that readily available for normal industrial usage having, at the most, a concentration of thirty-five per cent. Enlisting the aid of the Elektrochemische Werke in Munich, he had eventually succeeded in obtaining a hydrogen peroxide propellant of a concentration as high as eighty per cent, and at the behest of the Versuchsanstalt für Luftfahrt (DVL), or German Aviation Experimental Establishment, he extended his development programme to include a small, well-calibrated hydrogen peroxide rocket of ninety pounds thrust for testing the dynamic characteristics in roll of various aircraft, the intention being to fire the rocket on one wingtip and record the time history of the roll displacement.

The success of this small Walter rocket, which was also tested as a means of boosting the take-off and climb rate of an He 72 Kadett training biplane, dispelled some of the scepticism which still surrounded any suggestion of applying rocket power to manned aircraft. Further trials with a more powerful Walter rocket motor beneath an Fw 56 Stösser were sufficiently impressive to convince Dr Adolf Baeumker, Chief of the Research Department of the Air Ministry, that the development of such power plants for assisting the take-off of heavily-laden bombers and as prime movers in high-speed research airplanes was thoroughly worth pursuing.

Thus, in 1936, with the support of Dr Baeumker's Department, Walter began work on the HWK R I (Hellmuth Walter – Kiel – Rakete I), a rocket motor of what was later to become known as the 'cold' type, relying on the thrust obtained from the decomposition products of the hydrogen peroxide. (Some years later a second fuel was to be added to burn with the resulting oxygen and produce the bi-propellant or 'hot' type rocket motor.) Its fuel was eighty per cent hydrogen peroxide plus oxyquinoline or phosphate as a stabilizer, this being known as T-Stoff (although, with minor variations, it was also known as Auxilin, Aurol, and Ingolin), and an aqueous solution of calcium permanganate known as Z-Stoff, and the anticipated thrust was 860-880 pounds.

Meanwhile, the rocket motor of 650 pounds thrust that had been under development at Kummersdorf had been carried to a stage of comparative reliability, and Wernher von Braun, now thoroughly convinced of the potential of the liquid-fuel rocket as an aircraft prime mover, had succeeded in obtaining the fuselage of an old Junkers A 50 Junior light plane beneath which the rocket motor was attached. The spherical methyl alcohol and liquid oxygen tanks were installed in the fuselage itself, the operating levers and switches for the rocket motor were mounted in the cockpit, and the entire contraption was rigidly attached to a test stand.

Von Braun insisted on running the first firing trials himself, but the relatively light metal structure of the fuselage of the elderly Junkers tourer was ill fitted to withstand the strains and stresses imposed by 30-second bursts of rocket power. However, at least the rocket motor did not explode, and Ernst Heinkel, always receptive to ideas that promised an advance in technology, had already agreed to donate to the experimental programme the fuselage of an He 112 fighter, and also to lend von Braun the services of one of his best engineers, Walter Künzel, and a small team of riggers. With all possible secrecy, the He 112 fuselage, complete with wing centre section and undercarriage, and the Heinkel team led by Künzel, arrived at Kummersdorf at the beginning of 1936. The liquid oxygen container was installed ahead of the cockpit with the methyl alcohol tank behind the pilot's seat, and the rocket motor itself was sited immediately aft with the combustion chamber in the extreme tail, which was jacked up so that the exhaust gases were not directed obliquely downwards.

The first tests were conducted by remote control, the rocket motor being ignited from an observation post that had been built behind a thick concrete blast wall. Once they had overcome the initial problem of developing a combustion chamber, or 'pot' as it was known at Kummersdorf, capable of withstanding the immense pressures to which it was subjected, progress was rapid. Nevertheless, the first He 112 fuselage was totally destroyed by an explosion, and a second fuselage suffered the same fate. But despite the underlining by these accidents of the hazardous nature of the experiments, von Braun believed that the major

Wernher von Braun, who proposed the rocket-driven interceptor

difficulties had been overcome, and that the risk of testing the rocket motor in flight was justified.

He had already enlisted the services of a pilot, Erich Warsitz, who had gained some experience of test flying at the Air Ministry's Flight Test Centre at Rechlin, and persuaded Heinkel to provide a completely airworthy He 112. This was the fifth prototype of the fighter, the He 112 V5, and von Braun's idea was to install the rocket motor in the airframe in the same fashion as in the ill-fated static test specimens, retaining the Junkers Jumo 210 piston engine which he proposed should be run as a safety measure during take-off. The remote airstrip at Neuhardenburg, an unoccupied emergency field north-east of Berlin, was selected as the venue for the flight test programme, and early in March 1937, Warsitz eased himself into the cockpit, which was sandwiched between the liquid oxygen and alcohol tanks.

Everything was ready for what promised to be one of the most spectacular test flights since Orville Wright had lifted his stick, string and canvas contraption from a beach near Kitty Hawk, North Carolina, thirty-three years earlier. Warsitz fastened his seat straps, went through the usual checks, and started the Jumo engine. Once the Jumo had warmed up and was running evenly, he turned his attention to the rocket motor, and, carefully following von Braun's instructions, waited for the dials to register the correct tank pressures before cautiously pushing forward the lever that would ignite the rocket motor. Instantly, the stationary aircraft was ripped apart by a tremendous explosion. The heavy Jumo engine was flung high into the air, and pieces of the airframe were scattered far and wide. Horror-stricken, von Braun, Künzel, and other spectators ran towards the cloud of smoke hovering over the spot where, seconds before, the He 112 V5 had stood poised for take-off.

Miraculously, Warsitz had been flung clear of the aircraft, and had escaped with no more than minor cuts and contusions, and a few days later he was back at Marienehe pleading with Heinkel to provide yet another He 112 in order that the experimental programme could continue. Even Ernst Heinkel was now beginning to wonder if von Braun was not somewhat premature in his belief that the liquid-fuel rocket motor had reached a sufficient stage of reliability to warrant a further attempt to test it in flight, but he nevertheless acceded, and furnished a further He 112 prototype, this being a later B-series airframe with a Daimler-Benz DB 600 engine. The airframe was speedily adapted to accommodate the rocket motor and its fuel, with the tanks containing sufficient liquid oxygen and alcohol for a burning time of ninety seconds. Flight testing had begun before the end of April, but somewhat more caution was exercised in the first phase of the flight testing than had been apparent in the previous month's abortive attempt at rocket flight, and the modified fighter took off on the power of its DB 600 engine with the rocket unlit.

During the first flight, Warsitz climbed to some 2,600 feet, levelled off and, at 190 mph, cut the DB 600 and ignited the rocket motor. Warsitz subsequently commented that when he switched on the rocket it was as though he had been 'kicked in the backside'. Within a few seconds the airspeed indicator had read 250 mph and the aircraft had begun a shallow climb. The indicator needle continued to move around the dial . . . 260 . . . 270 . . . 280 . . . 285 mph, until at the end of the thirty seconds burning time which the propellant fuel provided, the rocket cut out. That the test had been a success there was no doubt. For the first time an aircraft had been propelled in flight solely on the power of a liquid-fuel rocket, and von Braun and his team were understandably jubilant.

The He 112 was experimentally flown with a rocket motor in its tail

A further flight with partly-filled tanks was successfully made, and it was concluded that Warsitz had now gained sufficient experience to fly the aircraft fully tanked up. The test went smoothly enough, and Warsitz had switched off the rocket motor and was turning towards the airfield when, to the dismay of the onlookers, the nose of the aircraft went down and Warsitz made a wheels-up landing in the scrub alongside the strip. After switching off the rocket, Warsitz had smelled burning, and the cockpit had filled with smoke. Believing the tail of the aircraft to be on fire, he had released his harness and pushed open the canopy in readiness to jump, and only then realised that his altitude was barely 1,000 feet and that he had no option but to crash land. He had hurriedly scrambled from what he believed to be a burning plane, and discovered, to his chagrin, that the only damage it had suffered had been caused during the landing. It was subsequently ascertained that the tongue of flame from the tailpipe, which, without developing power, continued for a few seconds after the rocket had been switched off, had been drawn into the interior of the aircraft by the airstream created in the fuselage during flight. The effect had been more alarming than dangerous.

Künzel and his team quickly repaired the aircraft, and in June a further series of tests began, in which Warsitz took off with both the DB 600 and rocket motor operating simultaneously. These tests revealed dramatically the phenomenal rate of climb with which an auxiliary rocket motor could endow an otherwise orthodox fighter, and understandably aroused the interest of the Air Ministry's Technical Department – interest which would prove not entirely beneficial to the main aim of evolving a pure rocket-propelled, high-speed aircraft. For some inconceivable reason, Warsitz's spectacular take-offs using both power plants diverted main Air

Ministry interest towards a development which, so far as von Braun and his co-workers were now concerned, was very much a side issue – the use of rockets as auxiliary power to assist overloaded aircraft to take off.

However, before the end of June, Warsitz had taken off on rocket power alone, had levelled off and flown around the field at high speed with the tail of the He 112 streaming fire, and had then glided in to a perfect landing. It had at last been proved that controlled flight from take-off to landing without the aid of an airscrew was possible. It was to be admitted that rocket-driven aircraft had in effect flown during the late 1920s, but some stretch of the imagination was necessary to claim that their flights had been controlled in anything but the broadest sense.

By this time, it could be seen that, as an aircraft prime mover, Hellmuth Walter's hydrogen peroxide rocket held greater immediate promise than the rocket developed at Kummersdorf. Not only was it simpler and apparently more reliable, it made no substantial demands on liquid oxygen, the availability of which was at that stage strictly limited. Furthermore, Walter was well advanced in the development of a pump system intended to replace compressed air for T-Stoff feed, which promised major thrust increases.

In the years between the World Wars the prestige to be gained by an aircraft manufacturer whose product had succeded in establishing a new international aviation record led to constant rivalry. The ultimate speed record was, by its very nature, the most coveted of these records, and it was on this prize that Ernst Heinkel had set his sights when, in the autumn of 1937, he first discussed with von Braun and Warsitz the possibility of designing a high-performance airplane specifically for rocket power. Heinkel already had plans for an attempt on the record with a special variant of a new fighter, the He 100, which had reached an advanced stage in construction at Marienehe, and which was in fact destined to gain for Germany and hold briefly the record at

463.92mph some eighteen months later. However, a specially-designed aircraft fitted with a sufficiently powerful liquid-fuel rocket could perhaps raise the record beyond the tantalising 1,000 kilometres per hour (621mph) mark, and this possibility represented a challenge that Heinkel was unable to resist.

Discussions with Hellmuth Walter had elicited the fact that he anticipated being able to offer within a year a rocket motor affording at least 1,300 pounds of thrust for a weight of less than 220 pounds. This was rather less than the 2,000 pounds of thrust promised by von Braun for the rocket then under development at Kummersdorf, but there seemed little likelihood of the more powerful unit being available for at least two further years. Unlike an orthodox piston engine, a rocket motor did not dictate a minimum size for the airframe in which it was to be installed, and after a series of conferences with the principal members of his design team, Heinkel concluded that the sort of performance at which he aimed could only be achieved by literally tailoring the aircraft to fit the pilot whose unenviable task would be to fly it – Warsitz! Evenso calculation suggested that every pound of thrust that could be squeezed from the more powerful von Braun rocket would be needed to approach 1,000 kilometres per hour.

Heinkel's brief was thus to produce the smallest possible airframe that could be wrapped around a 6ft 1in pilot, and under the overall supervision of Heinrich Hertel, Heinkel's Technical Director and Chief of Development, Walter and Siegfried Günter, probably the most talented and imaginative designers in the German aircraft industry before the war, conceived an aerodynamically clean cantilever monoplane which, in appearance, was orthodox in all

The He 176 was the first aircraft powered solely by a liquid rocket

but its size. The fuselage measured only three-quarters of an inch more than seventeen feet from nose to tail-pipe orifice, and at its broadest point it was barely twenty-eight inches wide. Many years later, Heinkel was to say that Warsitz found the cockpit more than a little cramped if he forgot to take his wallet from his pocket. The maximum depth of the fuselage was hardly more than three feet, and it was therefore necessary for the pilot to adopt a semi-recumbent position in the cockpit, reaching along to the rudder pedals in the extreme nose, and holding the stick between his knees, which were virtually level with his shoulders. A symmetrical wing profile was chosen in the light of the existing state of knowledge concerning high-speed flight, and the semi-elliptical wing spanned a mere 16ft 5in and afforded a gross area of only 58.12 square feet.

Hans Regner was assigned responsibility for detail design, and it was decided to build two prototypes, the first of which, for relatively low-speed trials, was intended for the Walter rocket motor, and the second of which was the high-speed machine with the more powerful von Braun unit. In order that the test programme should commence at the earliest opportunity, the first prototype was to be completed without the more sophisticated features of the second aircraft, construction of which was only to begin once full low-speed handling trials had been completed with the more primitive initial machine. Thus, whereas the definitive high-speed aircraft was intended to have fully-retractable mainwheels which were to be raised vertically into wells on each side of the hydrogen peroxide tank, the low-speed prototype had a fixed tricycle undercarriage, the main members being attached by cantilever legs to the forward fuselage bulkhead and having a track of only twenty-eight inches. Owing to the limited CG travel a fixed tail-skid was also provided, the intention being that

the aircraft should rest on this until the pilot entered the cockpit, his weight being sufficient to tip the aircraft on to its nosewheel.

At the comparatively low speeds that were to be expected with the first prototype, it was not anticipated that the pilot, who was to be seated in an open cockpit with his head barely protruding above the cockpit sill, would experience serious difficulty in evacuating the aircraft if necessary, despite his semi-recumbent position. The second prototype was another matter, however. At the speeds which it was hoped would be attained by this tiny rocket-driven plane, it was forseen that in an emergency escape for the pilot would be impossible by conventional means. After some experimentation, an ingenious scheme was devised which envisaged the arrangement of the entire fuselage forward of the main bulkhead as a detachable capsule. Separation from the remainder of the aircraft was to be aided by means of a compressed air device, and a parachute attached to the capsule was to be deployed automatically after separation, slowing the capsule sufficiently to permit the pilot to jettison the canopy, bail out and complete the descent in orthodox fashion by means of his personal parachute.

Several examples of the proposed cockpit capsule were eventually to be constructed, fitted with a variety of recording instruments and dummies of similar stature to that of Warsitz, and jettisoned from an He 111 bomber at altitudes between 20,000 and 23,000 feet in order to ascertain the chances of the pilot surviving. From these tests it was subsequently concluded that the revolutionary scheme was perfectly feasible, and that, always provided a situation did not develop preventing separation, the odds on the pilot's survival were acceptable.

Heinkel's development of the rocket-driven aircraft was a purely private venture, enjoying no official backing or encouragement, and when actual construction of the first prototype began late in 1937, it became necessary that the Air Ministry be informed fully on the stage reached with the project. Neither surprise nor particular interest was evinced in official circles. The Technical Department, which officially assigned the project the designation 'He 176', still saw the rocket motor as a device for aiding the take-off of overloaded aircraft, or at most, as an auxiliary unit to boost for brief periods the performance of conventional pursuit aircraft, but not as a prime mover for a manned aircraft.

Dr Lorenz, the assistant to Dr Baeumker of the Air Ministry's Research Department, was not so convinced that the application of rocket power to manned aircraft was so limited, and was confident that research with manned rocket-driven aircraft was of more than academic interest. He also thought that the He 176 was too conventional in configuration to take full advantage of this unconventional form of propulsion, and that a tailless design was best suited for rocket power. Alexander M Lippisch, who nearly a decade previously had been responsible for the design of the rocket-driven Ente glider, undoubtedly possessed more experience than any German designer with the tailless configuration, and was therefore approached by Dr Lorenz with the proposal that an airframe based broadly on the design of the piston-engined Delta IVc should be evolved for flight testing of Walter's HWK R I hydrogen peroxide rocket motor at speeds up to 280-310mph.

Until the previous year, the future of the tailless aircraft configuration in Germany had hung by a thread as a result of a series of accidents, and until the début of the Delta IVc, which provided positive proof that the tailless configuration did not of necessity possess inherently dangerous handling characteristics, Lippisch had been viewed almost universally as a crank, with the pundits loudly

declaiming that an aircraft without a tail must of necessity be unstable. Lippisch's tailless Delta series had certainly suffered a checkered career. The original Delta IV had been built in 1932 by the Gerhard Fieseler Werke as the Fieseler F 3 Vespe (Wasp), with the aim of entering this highly unconventional airplane in the Europarundflug to be held that year. The Vespe (alias Delta IV) featured a broad-chord wing with a sharply tapered leading edge, and a straight trailing edge occupied entirely by flaps and elevons. A small canard foreplane had been provided, together with endplate wingtip vertical surfaces, and the plane had been propelled by a pair of 75hp Pobjoy 'R' seven-cylinder air-cooled engines, one mounted in the nose of the abbreviated fuselage as a tractor and the other at its extreme end as a pusher.

Gerhard Fieseler was undoubtedly the greatest German aerobatic pilot of his era, practising the *haute école*,

Ernst Udet, who was incensed by the demonstration of the He 176

but he possessed no experience of flying such unconventional aircraft as that designed by Lippisch, and, despite an agreement that the first tests of the Vespe would be undertaken by Lippisch's own pilot, Wiegmeier, Fieseler took the aircraft up for its maiden flight and promptly crashed. Lippisch had then repaired the damaged airframe, removed the foreplane and rear engine, and with the aid of a well-known sailplane pilot, Günther Groenhoff, had resumed testing the aircraft as the Delta IVa. From the outset, the aircraft had displayed execrable handling characteristics, and Groenhoff had crashed during a landing approach. This accident was promptly followed by the crash of Lippisch's earlier Delta III at Halle, when Wiegmeier unwisely attempted a so-called 'cavalier start', in which the mainwheels left the ground before the tailwheel, and stalled in. Lippisch in particular and the tailless configuration in general had been in bad odour.

Fortunately, Dr Walter Georgii of the Deutsches Forschungsinstitut für Segelflug (DFS), the German Research Institute for Gliding Flight at Darmstadt-Griesheim, had come to Lippisch's rescue, had taken the Delta IVa under the wing of the Institute, and had rebuilt it as the Delta IVb DFS 39). The wing platform had been drastically revised, with sweepback applied to the wing trailing edges, and the endplate vertical surfaces had been supplanted by wingtips embodying marked anhedral. Dihedral had been applied to the wing roots, and fixed slats had been introduced above the leading edges of the inboard wing sections. Successful trials had been conducted with the Delta IVb as a single-seater, and a second airframe had been completed as the two-seat Delta IVc, which had been awarded a full certificate of airworthiness in 1936. It was this aircraft that it was now proposed should be adapted to take a rocket motor.

Although Lippisch had been somewhat disheartened by the lack of success that had been enjoyed by his Ente, he had nevertheless maintained contact with developments in rocketry, and had made a thorough study of the problems of rocket-powered flight. He was not therefore greatly surprised by Dr Lorenz's proposals, and, after being apprised of the stage in rocket motor development attained by Hellmuth Walter, embraced them with some enthusiasm. Lippisch's rocket-driven aircraft was simply referred to as 'Project X', a contract was drawn up by the Research Department to cover its development, and work began in utmost secrecy in a specially-built and closely-guarded room at the DFS.

In view of the nature of the power plant to be used for Project X, an all-

One of Lippisch's early (1932) projects destined to lead to the Komet

metal fuselage was considered to be a prerequisite, and as suitable facilities for its construction did not exist at Darmstadt-Griesheim, this work was sub-contracted to Ernst Heinkel at Marienehe on the instructions of the Research Department, while the DFS retained responsibility for construction of the wooden wings. Free-flight model tests and extensive wind tunnel investigations soon revealed that directional stability and yaw-roll characteristics would be much improved by the use of a swept wing without dihedral, and with a centrally-mounted vertical stabilizer. The end-plate vertical surfaces used by the Delta IVc had tended to cause some flutter at the upper end of the performance scale, as they were aft of the elastic axis of the wing, and tended to change their hinge-moment characteristics with the span load on the wing due to variations in lift conditions.

The results of wind tunnel testing after these changes had been made were exceptionally good, but by now the Project X differed so radically from the Delta IVc that Lippisch decided to design a small powered-glider of similar configuration to serve as an aerodynamic test bed. Spanning 34ft 9in, and having an overall length of 23ft 7½in, this flying test bed received the designation DFS 194, and it was intended that a light air-cooled engine be mounted in the rear portion of the fuselage, driving an airscrew aft of the vertical stabilizer by means of a short extension shaft. By the end of 1938, however, Alexander Lippisch was suffering constant interference through his work being harassed by unnecessarily harsh security restrictions, and the plan under which Ernst Heinkel was to build the Project X fuselage had proved unworkable. In desperation, Lippisch elected to take on responsibility for building the entire aircraft, but this decision, together with certain policital considerations, necessitated leaving the DFS and entering the aircraft industry proper.

Some negotiations with Willy Messerschmitt had led to an invitation to Lippisch to join the Messerschmitt AG at Augsburg-Haunstetten. This invitation was accepted and, on 1st January 1939 Lippisch and twelve co-workers arrived at Augsburg-Haunstetten to form Department 'L' ('L' indicating 'Lippisch'). The transfer of Project X from the DFS to Messerschmitt brought it within the orbit of the Technical Department of the Air Ministry, by no means favourably disposed towards either rocket-propelled aircraft or aircraft of tailless configuration, and this change was accompanied by the allocation of the designation Me 163 to the project. Shortly afterwards, the nearly-completed DFS 194 airframe was transferred from Darmstadt-Griesheim to Augsburg-Haunstetten, and somewhat surprisingly in view of the basically wooden structure of the fuselage, the decision was taken to discard the piston engine and adapt the DFS 194 to take the HWK R I rocket.

In the meantime, Heinkel had completed the first He 176 at Marienehe, and in the late summer of 1938 the dismantled airframe had been sent to the secret new experimental centre at Peenemünde to which Walter Dornberger and Wernher von Braun had transferred their activities a few months earlier. This establishment, on the Baltic coast, was operated jointly by the army and the Luftwaffe, and most of the army staff formerly engaged on rocket development at Kummersdorf had already been transferred to this closely-guarded establishment. Owing to the secrecy surrounding the He 176, it had not been possible to perform any trials at Marienehe, and it was proposed that Warsitz should get the feel of the controls of this somewhat primitive-looking little monoplane while it was towed at speed, along the superbly smooth stretches of sand beach between Swinemünde and Usedom, behind Heinkel's 7.6-litre Mercedes.

After the tow-car itself had bogged down in soft sand-patches on several occasions, it was concluded that further towing trials of this nature could not be conducted without risk of damage to the aircraft, and that high-speed taxying trials should therefore be delayed until after installation of the rocket motor. This, the HWK R I-203, differed from the R I intended for installation in Lippisch's aircraft in having a pump for the T-Stoff feed, and was expected to provide some 1,320 pounds of thrust. That the Walter motor was hardly less temperamental than that developed by von Braun and his team had already been graphically illustrated when an R I-203 had exploded while running on a test stand at Kummersdorf, destroying an entire building, and a similar accident was to take place shortly afterwards at the Luftfahrtforschungsanstalt (Aviation Experimental Institute) at Braunschweig-Volkenrode, Trauen. The Z-Stoff tended to clog the jets, and with insufficient quantities of the catalyst being supplied, the pressure and thrust fluctuated considerably, imbalance in the mixture of fuel fed to the combustion chamber involving the constant danger of explosion.

For the initial ground trials at Peenemünde-West it was intended that Warsitz would use short bursts of rocket power, progressively building up the speed until the control surfaces of the tiny airplane became effective. The fact that no means of varying the thrust of the rocket motor had then been evolved meant that the Walter engine either generated full thrust or no thrust at all, and Warsitz's first attempt to taxi the He 176 under power was almost his last. The effect of the rocket thrust on the little aircraft was so enormous that it shot forward like a bullet from a gun, snaking on its narrow-track undercarriage, and had Warsitz not had the presence of mind to immediately cut the power the aircraft would undoubtedly have ground looped. A technique for the high-speed runs along the main runway was eventually evolved, but as taxying speeds increased and the He 176 displayed no inclination to leave the runway, it became obvious, somewhat to the Heinkel team's embarrassment, that, with the power available, the diminutive wings (which were identical to those intended for the very much more powerful high-speed second prototype) generated insufficient lift to get the aircraft off the ground; that a redesigned wing employing a higher-lift section and possessing greater surface area would be necessary; and that even then the runway was likely to be too short to afford Warsitz a safety margin in the event of an aborted take-off.

Work began immediately on extending the runway westward almost a mile, and at Marienehe it was a case of 'back to the drawing boards' to design an entirely new wing. The redesigned wing eventually reached Peenemünde in the spring of 1939, and the test programme was resumed. The He 176 eventually succeded in staggering off the runway under power for the first time on 20th June 1939, in a flight which lasted fifty seconds and barely exceeded 170mph. The fact that the aircraft had at last flown was greeted with some jubilation by the Heinkel team. Hermann Göring's deputy, Erhard Milch, and the Luftwaffe's Chief of Aircraft Procurement and Supply, Ernst Udet, together with their respective retinues, promptly arrived at Peenemünde to witness the second flight. The Luftwaffe General Staff had already begun to think along the lines of a rocket-propelled interceptor fighter, but neither Milch nor Udet had previously displayed any interest in the potentialities of rocket propulsion. Both men were, after their own fashion, traditionalists, and they were obviously still sceptical of the He 176's ability to fly at all.

As soon as he had glanced at the tiny plane, the wings of which, despite having been enlarged, were still ex-

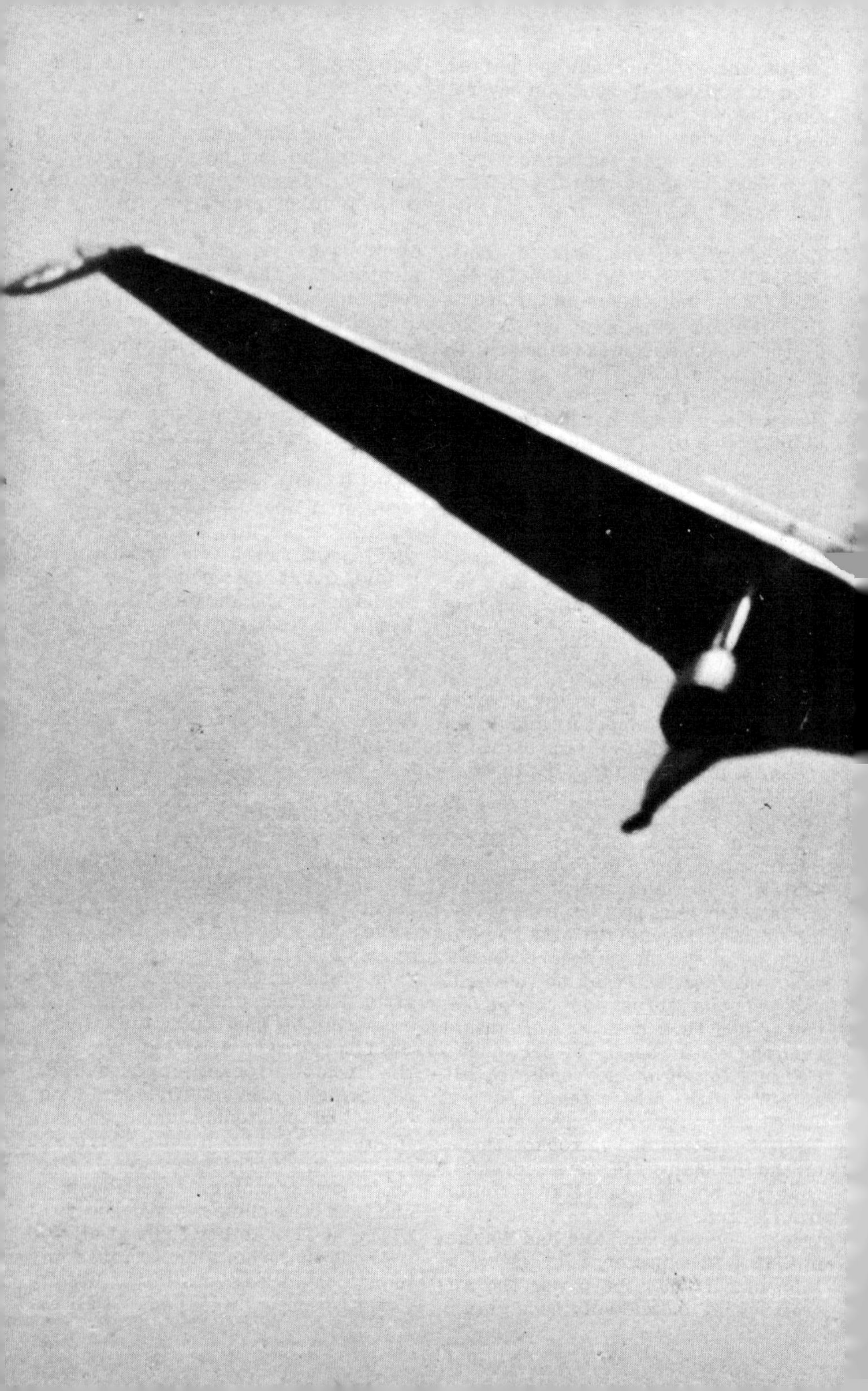

Ernst Heinkel and (right) Ernst Udet

tremely small, Ernst Udet turned to Warsitz and exclaimed, 'You want to fly with that? It has no wings . . . those are running boards!' Nevertheless, after a long run, Warsitz took off, flew somewhat shakily around the field, cut the rocket motor, made a steep gliding approach and touched down at high speed. Milch and Udet remained all too obviously unimpressed by this hair-raising demonstration. Indeed Udet, so incensed by what he considered a supreme example of design irrationality and a dangerous stunt lacking any practical application, declaimed, 'That is no airplane. Leave it alone! I forbid you to fly it again!' In vain Warsitz protested the case for the continuation of experiments with rocket-powered flight, of the previously undreamed of speeds that might now be within their grasp, but Udet remained unmoved. The hazardous stunt that he had witnessed had not fired his imagination. To him the He 176 was a highly volatile toy and nothing more, and as it was more than likely that Europe would soon be at war, it was his opinion that responsible aircraft manufacturers such as Ernst Heinkel should not be dissipating their efforts with toys at such a time.

It was true that the first tests with the He 176 had not met the more sanguine expectations of the Heinkel team, but at least they had proved that it would fly and were dismayed by Udet's attitude and his ban on the further testing of the aircraft. Ernst Heinkel hurried to the Air Ministry in Berlin to plead with Udet who half-heartedly withdrew the ban, but testing at Peenemünde had hardly been resumed when Heinkel was informed that no further tests with the He 176 were to be conducted before 3rd July, and that the aircraft must be at the Rechlin experimental centre on that date for a 'special demonstration'. Heinkel's hopes rose. Had the Air Ministry suddenly changed its attitude to rocket propulsion? On enquiring what this 'special demonstration' was in aid of, however, he was informed by Udet that there was to be a display of new aircraft types for the Führer. Udet added, as Heinkel subsequently related, 'The Führer must be shown something new, and I suddenly remembered your comical bird! If it can get around the airfield that will be good enough.'

At Rechlin, the Führer was accompanied by Göring, Milch, Udet, Jeschonnek, von Keitel and Jodl, and the demonstration of the He 176 by Warsitz was nothing if not spectacular. The tiny airplane gathered speed rapidly down the runway, Warsitz pulling the nosewheel off the ground almost abreast of the official party, and then literally rocketing up to about 2,500 feet. A tight circuit of the field under full power and Warsitz chopped the rocket motor, approaching the runway in a fast glide, apparently to land. Suddenly he relit the rocket motor, shot once more into the air, made a half-circuit under power using the remainder of his fuel, and finally landed. The Führer politely complimented Heinkel on the spectacular nature of the He 176, and then, somewhat surprisingly, asked, 'What does Warsitz get for this flight?' Göring's contribution was to turn to the test pilot, who had by now joined the group of spectators, and ask, 'Well Warsitz, what do you make of it all?' To this the pilot replied, 'I am convinced, Herr Reichsmarshall, that within a few years we will not see many military aircraft with airscrews!' To this Göring rejoined, with a note of condescension in his voice, 'Warsitz, you are something of an optimist.'

Warsitz was not alone in believing that there was a place in the inventory of the Luftwaffe for a rocket-propelled interceptor. On 6th July, three days after the demonstration of the He 176 at Rechlin, Wernher von Braun submitted to the Air Ministry a document expounding his ideas on a manned rocket-driven vertical-take-off interceptor, entitled 'Proposal for a High-performance Reaction-propelled Aircraft.' Based on experience gained at Peenemünde with the A 3 rocket, von Braun's scheme envisaged an interceptor possessing a take-off weight of 11,145 pounds propelled in climb by a rocket motor delivering 22,000 pounds of thrust, and launched vertically from two 20-ft guide rails. Von Braun calculated that the interceptor would climb vertically to 26,250 feet in fifty-three seconds under the control of a three-axis gyro system. On reaching operational altitude the pilot would cut the main rocket chamber and switch to an auxiliary chamber affording 1,600 pounds of thrust, simultaneously switching from gyro to manual control. A maximum speed of 447mph was anticipated on the thrust of the auxiliary chamber alone, and after exhausting its fuel the interceptor would glide back to its base and land on a skid.

Although the conventionalists in the Air Ministry's Technical Department said that von Braun's document read like science fiction, and that the entire concept was far too futuristic, the proposal was not dismissed out of hand, and as the Heinkel company at that time possessed the most experience with rocket propulsion, Dr Motzfeld, Heinkel's Development Director, was asked for his opinion on von Braun's proposals. Dr Motzfeld's report was unenthusiastic, commenting, 'The proposal raises several interesting ideas which could well be worth following up, but it will have practical meaning only when the designer succeeds in increasing the altitude attained on the main rocket chamber by several thousand metres, and in prolonging the flight endurance on the auxiliary chamber.' He added that, in his opinion, the degree of vertical climb efficiency provided by von Braun's rocket motor 'does not seem to me to afford any real tactical advantage.'

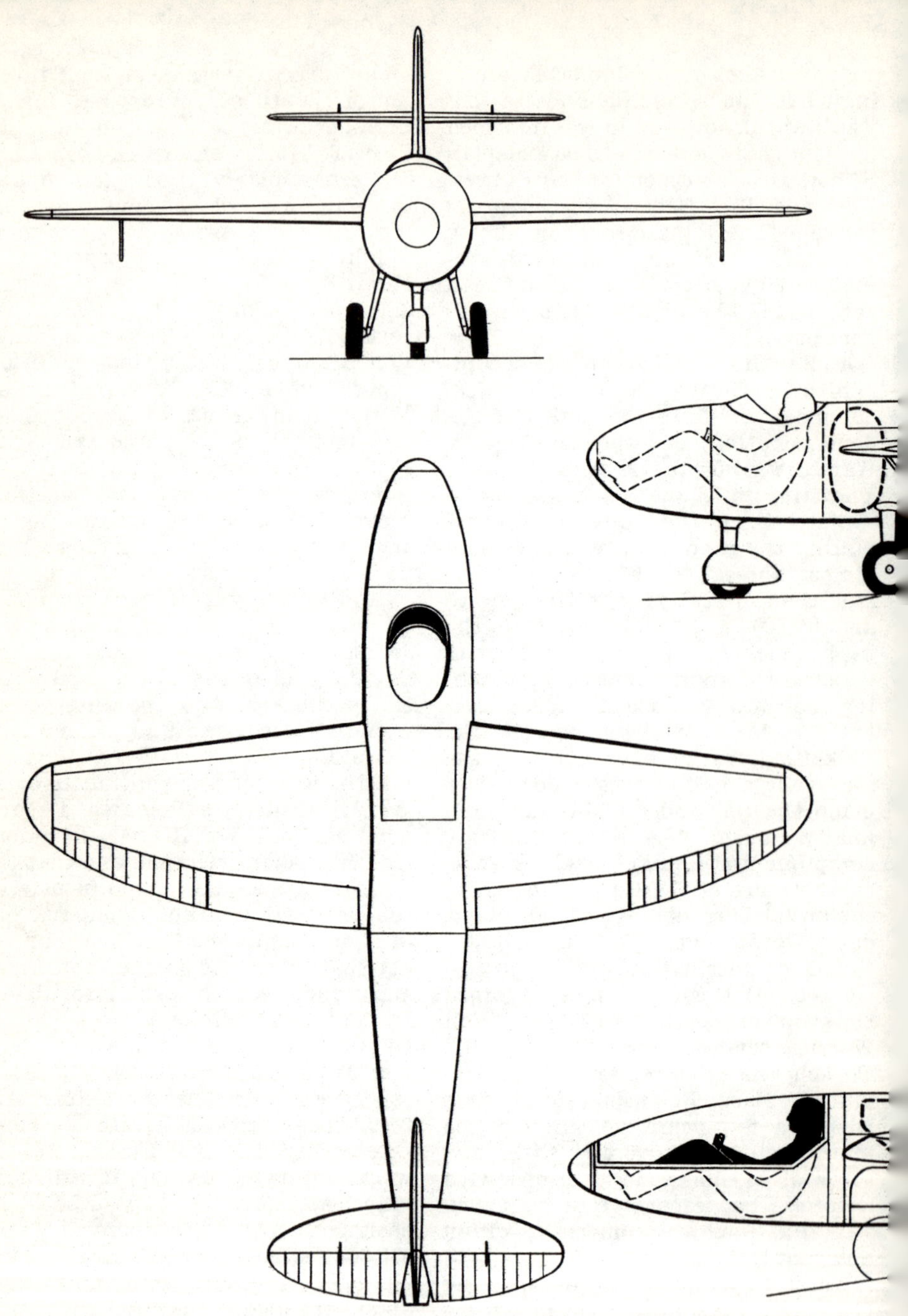

The tiny Heinkel He 176 was virtually tailored to the size of its pilot. The second prototype (illustrated by the lower sideview) was to have featured a more powerful rocket, an enclosed cockpit and a retractable under-carriage, but this model progressed no further than the drawing board

Eventually, von Braun's scheme was to be rejected by the Air Ministry as impracticable, although it captured the imagination of Erich Bachem, then Technical Director of the Gerhard Fieseler Werke, with results that were to be seen several years later. So far as the He 176 was concerned, the limited success achieved by this aircraft was in no small part responsible for the disinterest evinced in official circles in the rocket-propelled interceptor fighter concept, which, by the time the first shots of the Second World War were fired, had become something of a joke. Udet, Milch, and the Luftwaffe General Staff were convinced that the conflict would be won with the weapons already in their armoury; the more esoteric lines of development, if not actually banned, were actively discouraged.

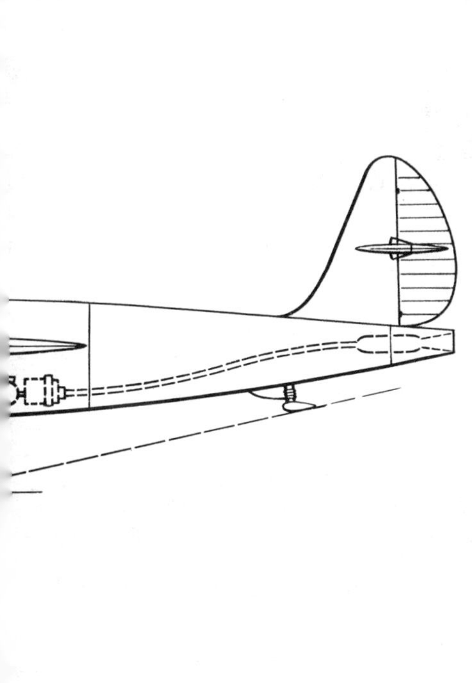

Permission for Heinkel to proceed with construction of the rather more sophisticated second prototype He 176 was withheld, and the first prototype was crated and sent to the Air Museum in Berlin where it was eventually to be placed on display as a whimsical example of aircraft development. In the event, its prospects as a museum attraction were to be ruined by an RAF bomb, and a decade later drawings and models depicting the much more advanced second airplane, which, with enclosed cockpit, retractable undercarriage, and much redesign, had progressed no further than the Marienehe drawing boards, were to appear and purport to depict the appreciably less ambitious aircraft that in fact actually flew at Peenemündo and Rechlin. Lippisch's Department 'L' at Augsburg-Haunstetten was to struggle on, its work being allocated the lowest possible priority, and when in September 1939 hostilities began, the entire future of the Me 163 hung by a thread, and there seemed little likelihood that the project would long survive the demise of the He 176.

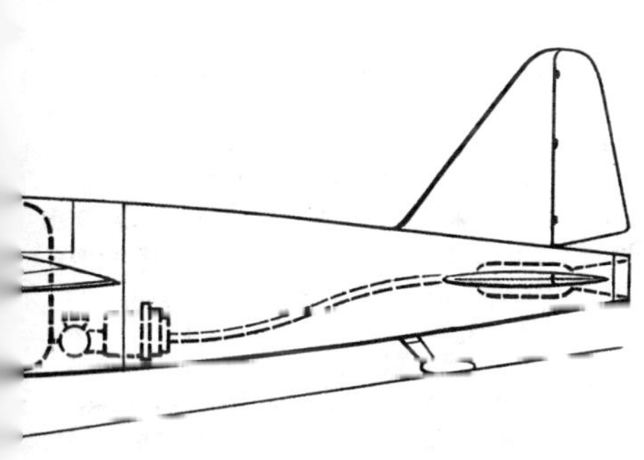

Meanwhile, further East . . .

Germany had not been alone in investigating the possibilities of rocket propulsion, and quite a comprehensive research programme had been proceeding in the Soviet Union. That the USSR was not disinterested in rocketry was, of course, well known. Indeed, a Russian, Konstantin Tsiolkovsky, born in the village of Izhevskoye in 1857, was widely accepted as the 'father of Rocketry and Astronautics', the measure of his genius being revealed by the fact that, as early as 1903, he had published a paper which was nothing less than the fundamental theory of the liquid-propellant rocket motor, even specifying the use of liquid oxygen and liquid hydrogen. Tsiolkovsky was purely a theorist, but his prognostications had had a profound effect on more practical men, prominent among them being Fridrikh Arturovich Tsander and Valentin P Glushko.

Rocket experimentation in the Soviet Union had, however, been enveloped by a cloak of secrecy of even tighter mesh than that thrown over all rocketry in Nazi Germany. The acronym 'RNII' had come to the notice of the Wehrmacht intelligence offices in Berlin from time to time, and had been loosely connected with experimental rockets, but reports of the testing of gyro-stabilized ballistic and winged rockets using liquid propellants, experiments with take-off assistance rockets, and the development of air-launched rocket missiles, were greeted with profound scepticism. In view of the strictly limited success that had attended German experiments in rocketry, the concensus of opinion in Berlin Intelligence circles was that if the Russians were conducting such experiments, Soviet aspirations far outstripped Soviet technology.

This opinion had little validity, for the RNII, or Rocket Scientific Research Institute, had been engaged in a rocket development programme far broader in base than that conducted in Germany. The RNII had been created in 1934 as a result of proposals made by Marshal Tukhachevsky, C-in-C of the Soviet Armed Forces, that work on rocket propulsion for military use being conducted independently by the GIRD (Rocket Propulsion Study Group) in Moscow and the GDL (Gas Dynamics Laboratory) in Leningrad should be coordinated. Tukhachevsky was convinced that the rocket had a major rôle to play in warfare, and his plan, first presented on 16th May 1932 and calling for the expenditure of five million roubles, had been approved by the People's Commissariat for Defence, the Narkomat Oborony, on 31st October 1933.

Separate teams had been formed from former GIRD and GDL personnel, each team concentrating its effort on a different aspect of rocketry, including the investigation of the use of such fuels as powdered aluminium, the auto-stabilization of rockets, the development of smokeless powder rockets with warheads as air-to-air and air-to-surface weapons and for surface-to-surface saturation bombardment, the continuation of trials with take-off assistance rockets, and the development of liquid-propellant rocket motors of both fixed and variable thrust.

The GIRD had been founded in 1931 under the aegis of the Osoaviakhim, the All-Union Society for Aviation and Chemical Warfare, the GDL having been created several years earlier, and from some aspects the work of the two organisations had followed parallel lines. At the GIRD, Fridrikh Tsander, who had built and tested the small OR-1 liquid-propellant rocket of eleven pounds thrust in 1929, had developed the OR-2 which, using jellied gasoline and liquid oxygen, and weighing forty pounds, provided 140 pounds of thrust. Simultaneously, at the GDL, Valentin Glushko had evolved the ORM-1 using alcohol and nitric acid, and delivering about 220 pounds of thrust. The OR-2 was fired on a test stand for the first time on 18th March 1933, but ten days later Tsander had died, and with him also died a scheme to install this rocket motor in a specially-designed glider, the RP-1 (Raketny Planer-1 or Rocket Glider-1).

In 1932, Tsander had collaborated with Boris Ivanovich Cheranovsky in the design of a suitable airframe to test the OR-2 rocket in flight. Cheranovsky had been working on tailless aircraft design since 1921, and had produced designs of both parabolic and trapezoidal wing planform, the latter being generally similar in concept to the Delta series developed in Germany by Alexander Lippisch. Cheranovsky's design intended to receive the OR-2 was a single-seat tailless monoplane with a wing of trapezoidal type spanning 39ft 7in, and featuring endplate vertical surfaces and a small central fuselage nacelle which accommodated the pilot in an open cockpit with provision for the rocket motor immediately aft. This aircraft, which carried the design bureau designation of BICh-11, was completed some months before the first firing tests with the OR-2 were conducted. However, the rocket motor revealed a somewhat erratic performance and unstable characteristics under test, and with Tsander's death enthusiasm for the installation of the OR-2 in a manned aircraft also died. Thus the BICh-11 (alias RP-1) had eventually flown with a conventional ABC Scorpion engine of 22hp, the OR-2 being confined to experimental winged and ballistic projectiles, the first of which had attained an altitude of 4,920 feet on 17th August 1933.

The ORM-2 rocket motor was progressively developed, and in its improved ORM-12a form it attained a thrust of 660 pounds in 1935, but no attempt was made to mount this unit in a manned aircraft, emphasis being placed on the potentialities of rockets as missiles, although the testing of take-off assistance rockets, first initiated by the GDL at the Komendantsky airfield, Leningrad, in September 1932 with a twin-engined Tupolev TB-1 bomber (No. 614), was continued. Interest in the possibility of using a rocket motor as a prime mover for a piloted airplane was strictly limited during the mid 1930s, and proposals to mount a small liquid-propellant rocket, the RDA using pump-drive for the liquid oxygen feed, in a specially-designed glider which was to have been known as the RP-2, had been abandoned.

During this period, Ivan T Kleimenov, the first director of the RNII and its chief scientist, devoted his primary attention to the perfection of an 82mm smokeless powder rocket as a potential air-to-air weapon and a 132mm rocket as an air-launched

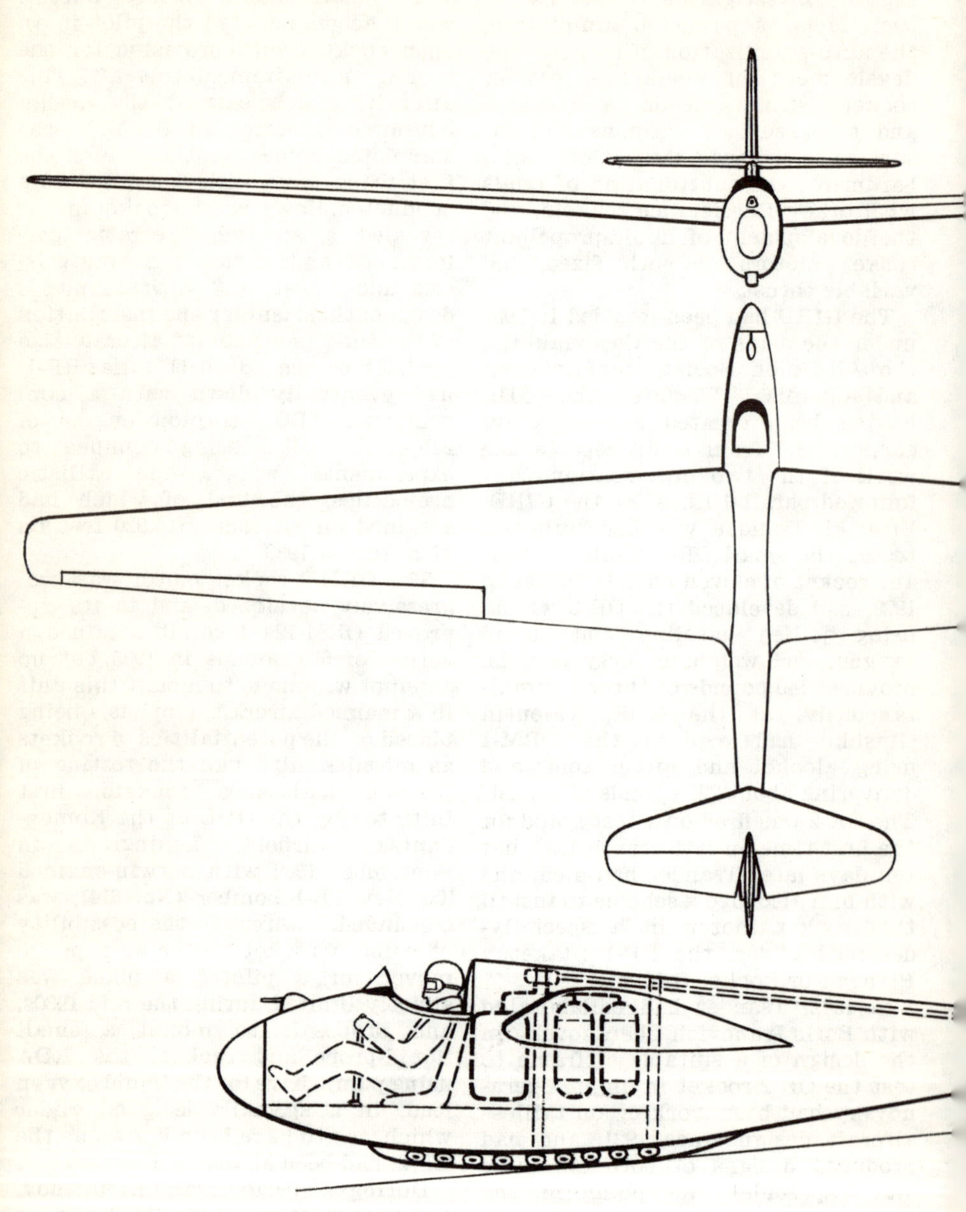

The first aircraft to be flown under rocket power in the Soviet Union was the RP-318, an adaptation of the Korolev-designed SK-9 sailplane. Powered trials with an RDA-1-150 rocket began at the end of February 1940, and provided the inspiration for development of Soviet rocket-driven interceptors

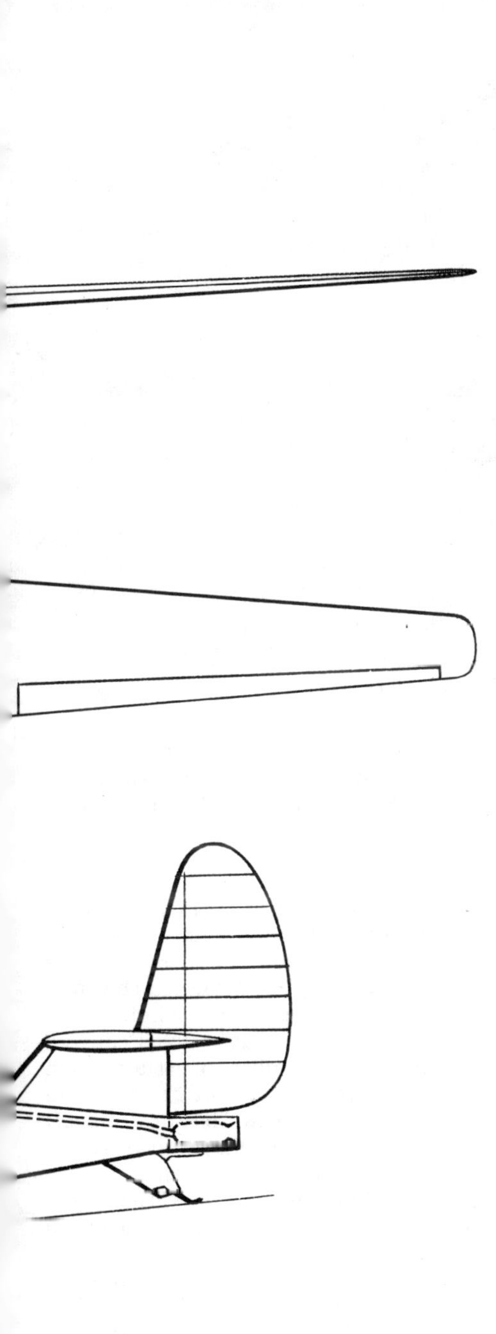

ground attack weapon. In this task he was aided by the chief engineer of the RNII, Georgi A Langemak, and after a successful series of ground launchings, the smaller-calibre rockets had been attached to racks beneath the wings of a Polikarpov I-16 fighter monoplane for air launching trials which had commenced in July 1937. The test pilot who had performed these trials was a certain Grigori Bakhchivandzhe who was later to have a closer association with rocket propulsion. Completed in December 1937, the trials had proved beyond doubt the practicability of the air-launched rocket missile as a weapon, and both 82mm and 132mm rockets were ordered into production as the RS-82 and RS-132, although by that time their originators, Kleimenov and Langemak, had fallen foul of the régime and had been arrested and executed, as indeed had Marshal Tukhachevsky who was largely responsible for the creation of the RNII.

In the meantime, Valentin Glushko had persisted with the development of liquid-propellant rocket motors using alcohol, gasoline or kerosene as fuel with nitric acid as the oxidant, with thrusts ranging from 176 to 1,320 pounds, and in 1937 serious consideration was again given to the installation of one of these power plants, the ORM-65, in a manned aircraft. Using kerosene and nitric acid, the ORM-65 gave a thrust of 385 pounds, and S P Korolev, the deputy scientific director of the RNII, suggested that an SK-9 sailplane of his own design should be adapted for this power plant. After a special committee had considered the suggestion, it was agreed that work on the conversion should be undertaken, and the task was assigned to two engineers, Aleksis Yakovlevich Shcherbakov and Arvid Vladimirovich Pallo, the rocket-driven version of the SK-9 sailplane being assigned the designation RP-318.

Work on the RP-318 proceeded

The B1 rocket-driven interceptor was initially flown as a glider (above and right). Water ballast simulated fuel and power plant

slowly owing to delays in achieving a satisfactory standard of reliability with the ORM-65 rocket, and meanwhile two other members of the RNII team, Leonid S Dushkin and Aleksei M Isaev, had developed a 330 pound thrust rocket which, as the RDA-1-150, used kerosene and nitric acid, or, as the RDK-1-150, alcohol and liquid oxygen. This unit was a major advance in that it featured controllable thrust, and it was proposed that the RDA-1-150 should supplant the ORM-65 in the RP-318, and that the RDK-1-150 should be mounted in a G-14 glider designed by Aleksis Shcherbakov. As the RDA-1-150 was favoured, priority was allocated to the development of this unit which was tested for the first time on 11th February 1939, the RDK-1-150 being abandoned.

The RDA-1-150 weighed 220 pounds, and this was installed in the extreme tail of the RP-318, the fuel and oxidant tanks being mounted immediately aft of the pilot's cockpit. With 165 pounds of fuel, which was sufficient for 100 seconds burning at full thrust, the RP-318 weighed 1,543 pounds. It had an overall wing span of 55ft 9in, and length from nose to tail was 23ft 10½in. The pilot assigned the task of flight testing the rocket-driven RP-318, Vladimir Pavlovich Fedorov, performed a number of trials with water ballast in place of the fuel and oxidant, and after satisfying himself that the handling characteristics of the airplane were acceptable, it was decided that the first powered flight test should take place on 28th February 1940.

Heavy snow had fallen throughout the night before the initial rocket trial, and the officer commanding the experimental establishment refused to sanction the test. In this decision he was overruled by the representative of the People's Commissariat of the

Aviation Industry, and Fedorov duly took off under tow by an old I-5 fighter biplane. The towline was dropped at 8,500 feet, and Fedorov ignited the rocket motor. Within five seconds the speed of the RP-318 had risen from 50 to 87mph and the aircraft was climbing at a rate of 590 feet a minute. At 9,500 feet, with the airplane still accelerating, the rocket motor exhausted the fuel, having run for 110 seconds, and Fedorov glided down to a perfect landing to complete the first flight to be made under rocket power in the Soviet Union.

Further successful trials were performed with the RP-318, two of which were witnessed by Aleksander Yakovlevich Bereznyak, an aerodynamicist working under Professor Viktor Fedorovich Bolkhovitinov at the Air Forces Academy. By this time, Dushkin and Isaev, assisted by A V Pallo, V A Shtokolov, and A P Sheptitsky, were engaged on the development of a substantially more powerful rocket motor based on experience gained with the RDA-1-150. Envisaged primarily as a propulsion unit for a heavy missile, and as a possible auxiliary motor for combat aircraft, this, the D-1A-1100, was expected to provide a thrust of 2,425 pounds, and when told of this new power plant by Aleksei Isaev, Bereznyak conceived the idea of designing a small target-defence interceptor around the rocket motor, totally unaware that a warplane of essentially similar concept was at that time being considered in Germany.

Bereznyak discussed his idea with Professor Bolkhovitinov who, after talking with Isaev, was so enthusiastic that he forwarded the scheme to the Narkomavprom, the People's Commissariat for the Aviation Industry, and, for good measure, wrote to Josef Stalin himself. The scheme

BI Rocket Fighter

1 Nose cone
2 Gun barrels
3 Air scoop
4 Kerosene cylinder
5 Compressed air cylinders
6 Gun cocking mechanism
7 Radio and battery bay
8 Breech of 20-mm ShVAK cannon
9 Ammunition tank (45 r.p.g.)
10 Rudder pedal
11 Instrument panel
12 Gunsight
13 Strengthened windscreen
14 Wing of stressed skin construction
15 Canopy jettison lever
16 One-piece canopy
17 Pilot's headrest
18 Ventilation panel
19 Pilot's seat and harness
20 Throttle control
21 Unarmoured bulkhead
22 Track for rearward-sliding canopy
23 Main compressed air cylinder
24 Main nitric acid cylinders
25 Stub aerial mast
26 Aerial
27 Oval section monocoque fuselage
28 Kerosene filters

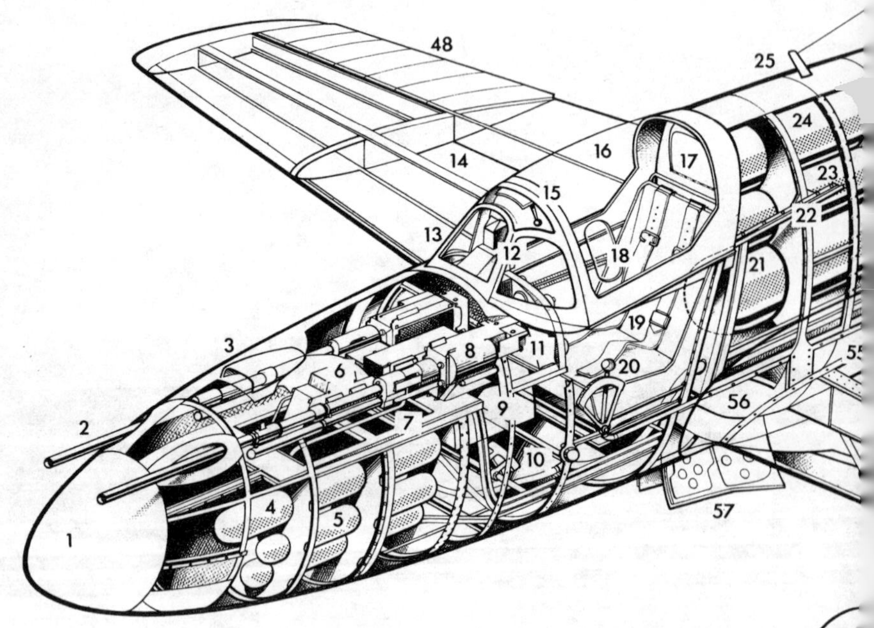

29	Nitric acid filters	44	Ventral fin
30	Pneumatically controlled valve	45	Semi-retractable tailwheel
31	Direct propellant tubes	46	Wing fillet
32	Injectors	47	Metal-skinned flap
33	Coolant pipes	48	Fabric-covered aileron
34	Dushkin D-1A-1100 rocket motor	49	Main spar
35	Rocket bearer/tailfin attachment	50	U/Carriage leg door
36	Tailfin construction	51	Mainwheel (low pressure)
37	Tailfin bracing	52	Main U/Carriage leg
38	Auxiliary endplate fins	53	Hydraulic retraction member
39	Rudder construction	54	Retraction pivot point
40	Exhaust chamber	55	Wing/fuselage attachment points
41	Combustion chamber	56	Wheel well
42	Exhaust orifice	57	Wheel well doors
43	Ventral fin bracing		

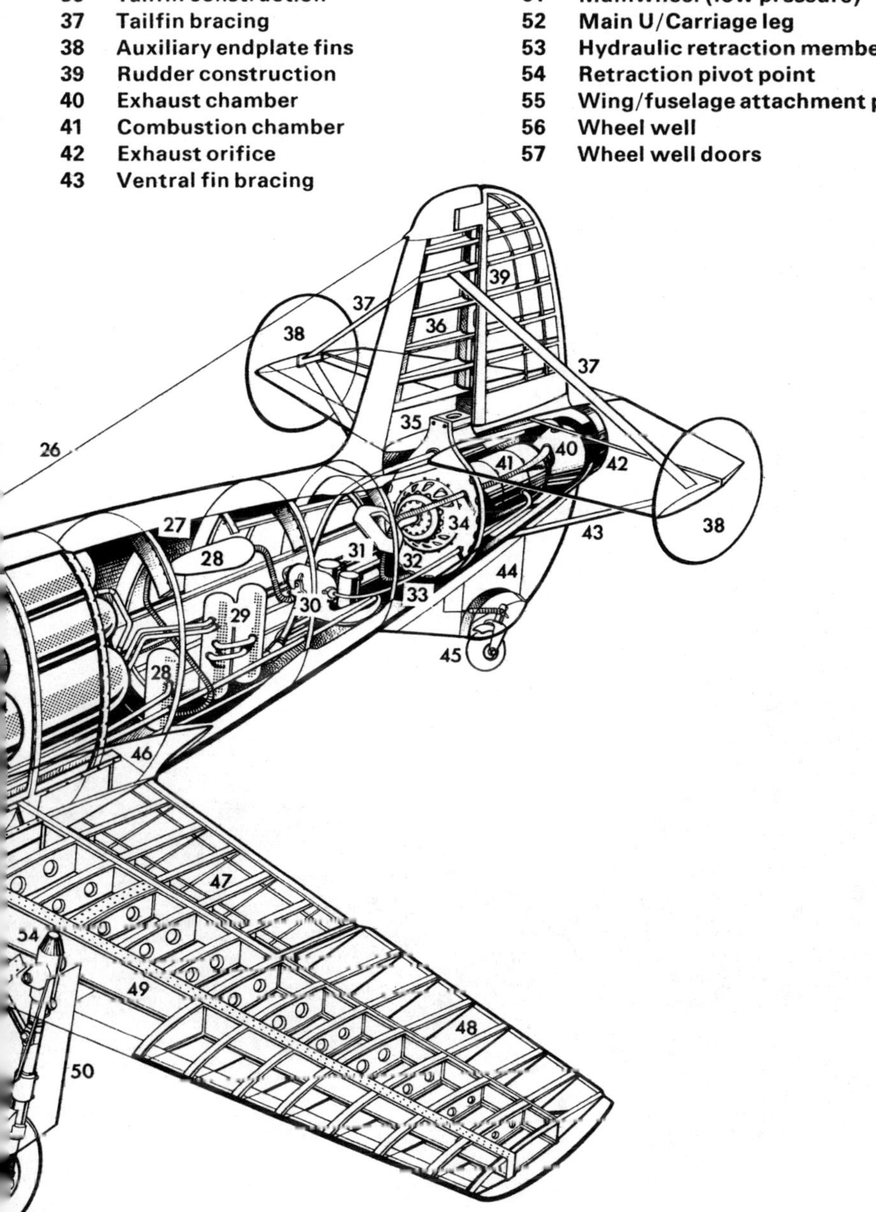

excited the interest of the Narkomavprom, and before the end of 1940 Bolkhovitinov's bureau had received the necessary authorisation to proceed with the design and construction of prototypes of a rocket-driven interceptor. Furthermore, an official requirement was drawn up around Bolkhovitinov's proposals to enable other design bureaux to consider this revolutionary concept.

The rocket-propelled fighter which took shape on the drawing boards at the Air Forces Academy under the supervision of Professor Bolkhovitinov was known simply as the BI (these letters standing for Bereznyak and Isaev who were primarily responsible for both the concept and the design), and the construction of several prototypes began simultaneously in a factory on the outskirts of Moscow. While these prototypes were still under construction, however, the assault on the Soviet Union had begun, and the rapid advance towards Moscow of the German forces dictated the hurried evacuation of the factory and the re-establishment of the BI team in a partly-completed iron foundry in the vicinity of Sverdlovsk, behind the Urals. Work was resumed on the construction of the prototypes despite the fact that, in the depths of the Urals winter, the assembly shop possessed no roof.

A special task force had been formed from personnel of both the original plant and the Air Forces Scientific Research Institute to pursue the completion and testing of the BI fighter with the utmost speed, its principal members being A Ye 'Roslyanov as chief engineer, with Arvid Pallo serving as his assistant, and, from the Institute, Colonel of Engineering M I Tarakanovsky who had been assigned responsibility for preparing the BI for its initial flight

Below: **The B1 interceptor could be fitted with either wheels or skis**
Right: **The B1 taking-off under rocket power**

test programme, A S Sorokin and A A Kolesnikov. Simultaneously with completing the BI prototypes, this task force had to roof the assembly shop and perform the first static tests with the D-1A-1100rocket motor, but despite the appalling conditions under which they were forced to work, the first BI airframe was completed for gliding trials during the early weeks of 1942.

The oldest active test pilot in the Soviet Union, B N Kudrin who had begun his career in 1916, had been assigned to the test programme as senior pilot, and performed the first gliding trials after being towed into the air behind a Pe-2 twin-engined light bomber. Four additional prototype airframes were completed almost simultaneously, and apart from some minor revisions to the control surfaces, the bracing of the horizontal stabilizer, and the strengthening of the windscreen, few changes resulted in the BI from the initial handling trials in glider form. The BI was, aerodynamically, a clean little airplane, apart from rather ungainly tail surfaces, and featured an oval-section metal monocoque fuselage, and a stressed skin wing of mixed construction comprising metal main and auxiliary spars and wooden ribs, the entire trailing edge being occupied by metal-skinned flaps and fabric-covered ailerons. The stabilizer included a substantial ventral fin to which was attached a retractable skid or wheel, and all movable surfaces were fabric covered. The main undercarriage members could be fitted with either wheels or skis, and retracted inwards hydraulically.

No armour protection was provided for the pilot who was accommodated in a very cramped cockpit, and enclosed by an aft-sliding single-piece hood. Provision was made for a pair of 20mm ShVAK cannon with 45 rounds per gun, and overall dimensions were extremely small, the wing spanning only 21ft 3in and having a gross area of a mere 75.35 sq ft, and the fuselage measuring 21ft from nose cone to rocket exhaust orifice. To achieve a satisfactory CG position, the kerosene tank was installed in the fuselage nose, ahead of the cockpit, together with the compressed-air cylinders for the hydraulic systems, the radio, and the armament, and the nitric acid tanks were positioned immediately aft of the cockpit, empty weight being 2,112 pounds and maximum loaded weight 3,710 pounds, the latter giving a wing loading of forty-eight pounds per square foot.

While gliding trials were in progress the second and third airframes were being prepared for tests with the rocket motor, but the programme had suffered two serious setbacks; Kudrin had been taken seriously ill, and his assistant, Grigori Bakhchivandzhe, who had been responsible for the first air launching trials of the RS-82 air-to-air rockets some four years earlier, had been injured during the ground testing of the first BI airframe to be fitted with the D-1A-1100 rocket Bakhchivandzhe had inadvertently opened the throttle too rapidly and the combustion chamber had exploded. Three of the test personnel had been burned by the oxidant, and Bakhchivandzhe had been thrown forward violently, hitting his head and suffering concussion. Although this accident meant a period in hospital, Bakhchivandzhe had recovered sufficiently to perform powered trials as soon as a further prototype was ready.

Taxying trials under power began during the first week of May 1942 at the Koltsova airfield, near Sverdlovsk, and during the last of these the BI left the runway and flew fifty-five yards in a straight line a few feet above the ground. Bakhchivandzhe reported that control response was favourable and that, as far as he could judge, the general handling characteristics of the airplane in fully loaded condition were acceptable, Major-General P I Fedorov, who had been assigned overall supervision of the test programme on behalf of the Air

Grigori Bakhchivandzhe was responsible for powered tests of the B1

Force, together with Professor V S Pyshnov, who had been attached to the BI team as an adviser, then prepared a detailed schedule for the first powered flight which it was decided should take place on 15th May.

The weather on the designated day proved extremely poor, with a low cloud base and strong crosswinds, but began to improve during the afternoon, and after performing a weather test in a Po-2 biplane, Bakhchivandzhe decided that the weather would have improved sufficiently by the early evening for the test to proceed. Accordingly, at 1900 hours Bakhchivandzhe ignited the rocket motor of the BI, the tanks of which had been filled with only sufficient fuel and oxidant for some three minutes flying at full thrust. With a stab of brilliant red flame patterned with shock waves, the small monoplane lurched forward, accelerated rapidly, and after a run of barely sixty yards lifted from the runway and climbed steeply to some 2,600 feet.

Bakhchivandzhe levelled off and, as speed built up, cut the rocket motor, circling the field in a high-speed glide. Turning in for the approach and lowering his flaps, the undercarriage having remained extended throughout the flight, Bakhchivandzhe misjudged the sink rate, held off too long, and hit the runway with considerable impact. The undercarriage collapsed but fortunately the aircraft suffered relatively minor damage. From take-off to landing the flight had lasted three minutes nine seconds, and the world's first genuine rocket-propelled interceptor had flown under full power. The pilot of the BI and the group of technicians who had anxiously watched its first powered flight had, of course, no idea that some 2,000 miles westward of Koltsova, at the experimental centre at Peenemünde which, at that time, was totally unknown to them, the

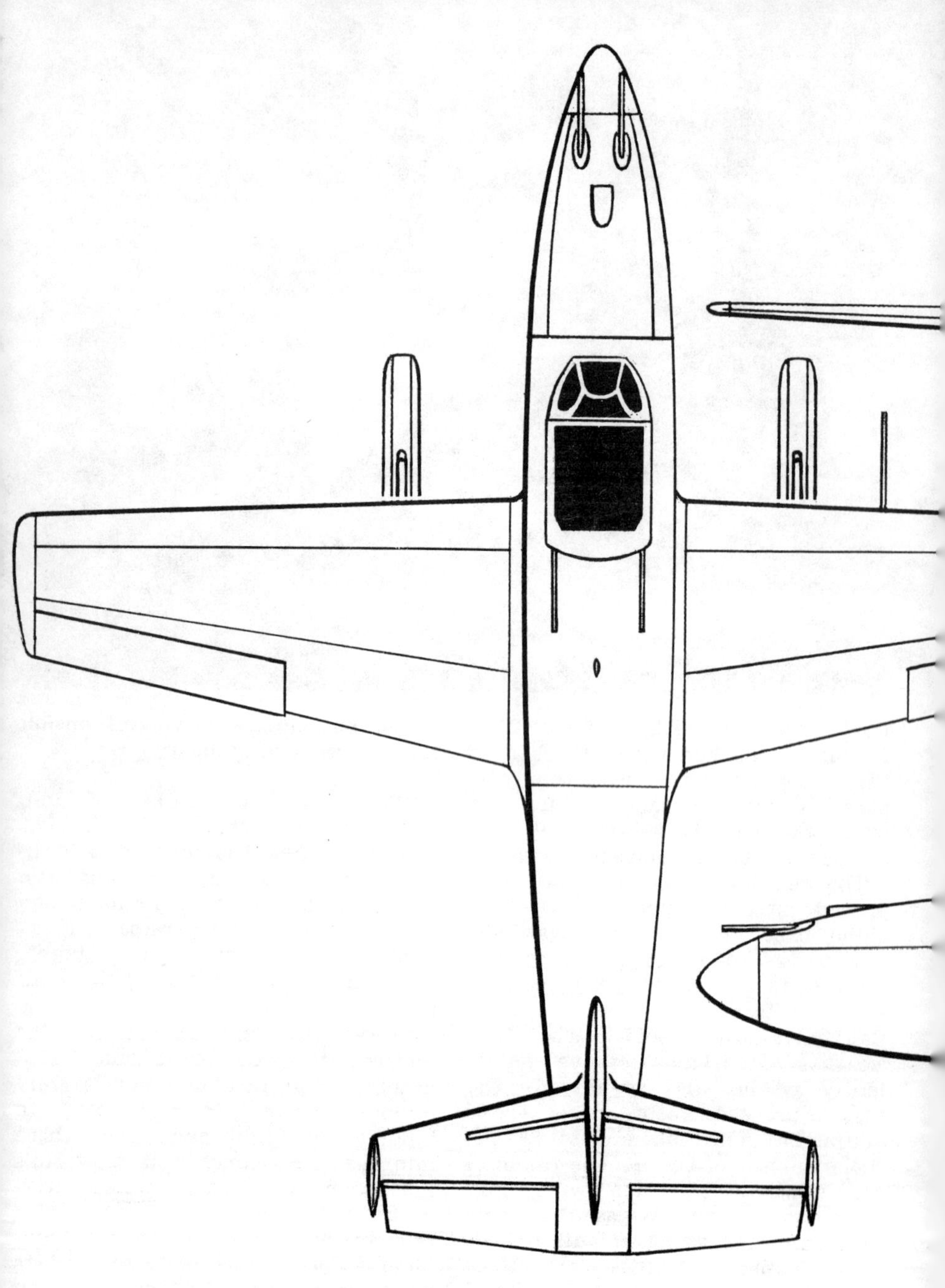

The B1 interceptor designed by Bereznyak and Isaev under the supervision of Professor Bolkhovitinov. It was the world's first combat airplane powered solely by a liquid-fuel rocket motor

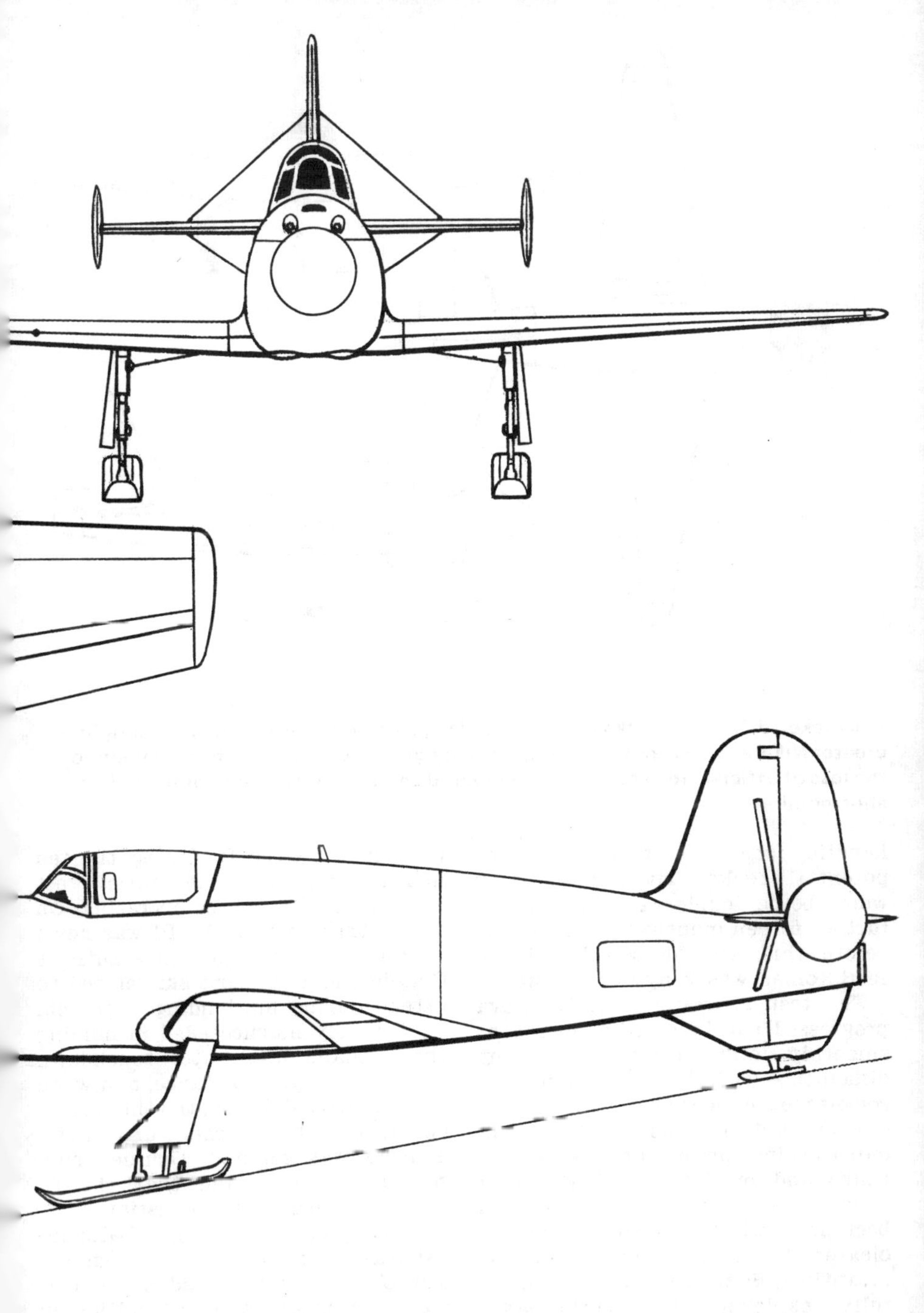

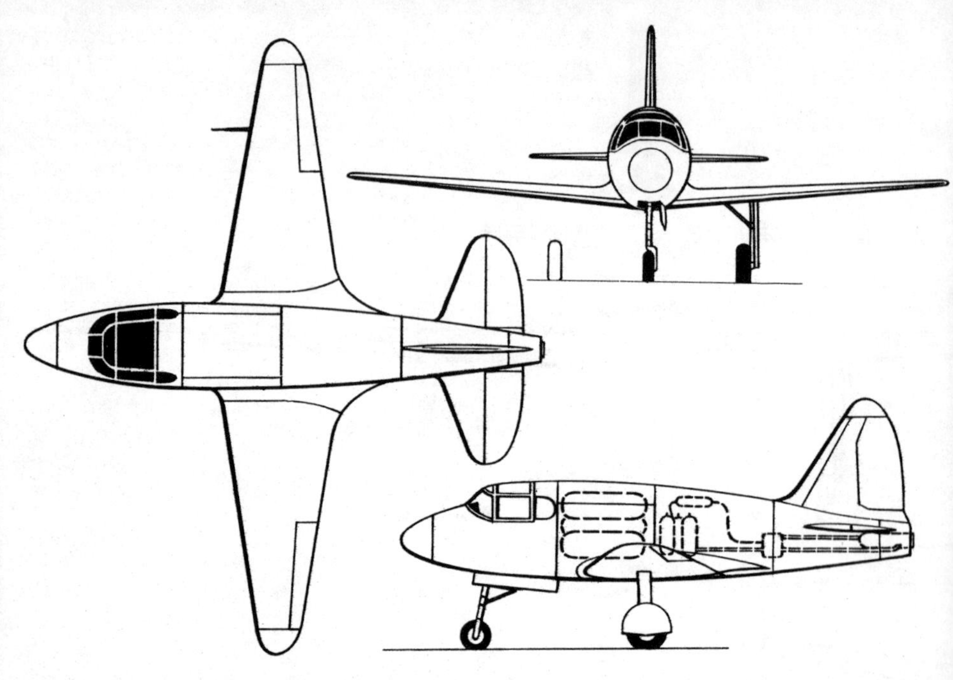

The rocket-driven Malyutka interceptor, designed by the bureau of veteran fighter creator Nikolai Polikarpov. The aircraft never got off the drawing board owing to the loss of official interest in rocket-powered combat aircraft following the BI's shortcomings

handling characteristics of another potential rocket-driven interceptor were being explored, although a further fifteen months were to elapse before this, the Messerschmitt Me 163B Komet, was to fly under power.

The test programme at Koltsova progressed slowly and by no means smoothly, often being delayed by difficulties with the temperamental rocket motor and its highly dangerous oxidant, not the least of these difficulties being corrosion of the oxidant tanks and pipelines, and almost a year passed before a second BI had been fitted with its rocket motor and cleared for flight testing. In the meantime, Bakhchivandzhe was carefully exploring the performance envelope of the little warplane, although, owing to various problems, only a half-dozen powered flights were performed by the BI during the ten months following the initial test with the rocket motor operating. On one of these flights the BI was flown by Lieutenant-Colonel Konstantin A Gruzdev, and the port ski refused to extend during his landing approach. Fortunately he succeeded in holding the airplane level after touchdown for a considerable distance, and when the port wing did drop, the thick snow cushioned the impact and little damage was suffered. Gruzdev subsequently commented that the BI 'flew like the devil's broomstick'.

On each successive flight Bakhchivandzhe attained a higher speed, and the BI team felt confident that it faced no insuperable difficulties in bringing the little warplane to operational status once the problems of the D-1A-1100 rocket motor had been overcome. During climbing trials the BI attained an altitude of 16,400 feet in thirty-five seconds and 32,810 feet in fifty-nine seconds, and it was calculated that a top speed of 600mph at sea level would be attainable, this rising to 614mph at 16,400 feet. Then, on 27th March 1943, tragedy struck the programme. Grigori Bakhchivandzhe took off on his seventh powered flight in the BI, intending to perform a high-speed run at an altitude of 6,560 feet. Witnesses of the test flight saw a sudden puff of dense black smoke from the tailpipe, and the aircraft, which it was estimated was travelling at a speed between 465 and 500mph, appeared to develop an uncontrollable nose-down pitch and had begun to break up before hitting the ground little more than a mile from the airfield. Bakhchivandzhe was killed instantaneously.

Pending the results of an investigation into this accident, work on an initial batch of fifty BI interceptors was suspended, and further flight testing, conducted by B N Kudrin, who had by now recovered from his illness, and M K Baikalov, was conducted under severe restrictions, although these pilots volunteered to simulate the test being performed by Bakhchivandzhe when he lost his life. Wind tunnel testing revealed the nose-down pitch at high speeds but no obvious means of overcoming the problem presented themselves, and, reluctantly, it was decided to abandon all further work on the BI. Only seven had been completed although some twenty additional machines were in an advanced stage of assembly.

The end of the BI programme was understandably accompanied by a total loss of official interest in the rocket-propelled interceptors designed to meet the official requirement that had been framed in 1940 around Professor Bolkhovitinov's original proposals. This loss of interest affected, in fact, only two projects: the I-302 that was being developed by a team led by M K Tikhonravov, who had worked at the GIRD in Moscow from its earliest days and had subsequently led one of the RNII teams working on liquid-propellant rocket motor development, and the Malyutka which was being evolved by a design collective supervised by veteran fighter designer Nikolai N Polikarpov. Shortly before further work on rocket-driven fighters was shelved in 1943, Tikhonravov's I-302 had begun gliding trials. Of thoroughly orthodox configuration, with a wing spanning 39ft 4½in, the I-302 was intended to carry an armament of four 20mm cannon, and was to have been propelled by the most powerful of a series of liquid-fuel controllable-thrust rocket motors that were being developed by Dushkin and Tikhonravov at the Scientific and Research Institute of the Air Forces (the NII V-VS – Nauchno-Issledovatelsky Institut V-VS). This, the NII-3, was expected to offer a maximum thrust of 3,310 pounds, and the take-off of the I-302 was to have been aided by two jettisonable auxiliary rocket motors. However, work on both the I-302 and the NII-3 was abandoned before airframe and power plant could be mated.

Nikolai Polikarpov's Malyutka was much closer in concept to the BI, although a rather more refined and from some aspects more sophisticated design. Barely larger than the BI, with a wing spanning only 22ft 11½in and an overall length of 19ft 8¼in, the Malyutka featured a fully-retractable tricycle undercarriage, provision for cabin pressurization, and an armament of two 20mm ShVAK cannon. Power was to have been provided by an NII-1 rocket motor of 2,645 pounds thrust. Design development of the Malyutka had begun in 1941, but progress had been slow owing to Polikarpov's failing health and the numerous other commitments of his design collective, and only a limited amount of work had been completed when the entire rocket fighter programme was abandoned.

From lowest to highest priority

Soviet interest in the potentialities of the rocket-propelled fighter concept which languished with the failure of the BI was to be revived several years later, but this renewal of interest was to be engendered not by developments in Soviet rocket technology but by work which, still far from fruition at the time the entire Soviet rocket fighter programme was cancelled, was taking place in the utmost secrecy in Germany, and the results of which were to be part of the USSR's inheritance following the downfall of the Third Reich.

While interest in rocket propulsion for aircraft was virtually non-existent in Germany during the first months of the Second World War, Alexander Lippisch and his small team at Augsburg-Haunstetten had quietly proceeded with their plans to install Hellmuth Walter's HWK R I rocket motor of 860-880 pounds thrust in the DFS 194, and suitably modified, the airframe had been transferred to Peenemünde-Karlshagen early in 1940 for the rocket motor to be actually installed. After some towed and free-gliding tests with ballast simulating the weight of power plant and fuel, the spring of 1940 saw the first 'sharp start', as take-offs with rocket power were soon to become known, with Heini Dittmar, who had been responsible for flight testing several of Lippisch's earlier designs, as pilot. Fully tanked-up, the DFS 194 weighed 3,527 pounds, with sufficient tankage available for 150 seconds of powered flight, and although only stressed for speeds of the order of 185-190mph, the DFS 194 was soon being flown at substantially higher speeds. In fact, the results of the initial flight test programme far exceeded the most sanguine expectations. Climb rate proved phenomenal, and Dittmar had soon exceeded 300mph in level flight and was eventually to reach 342mph.

Meanwhile, construction of two prototypes of the Project X, or Me 163 as it was by now known, had proved painfully slow, as, apart from Lippisch's own small team, labour from the Bf 110 assembly line in the main plant could only be spared during the infrequent slack periods such as occurred when there were delays in the arrival of components and sub-assemblies for the twin-engined fighter. However, the success recorded at Peenemünde by the DFS 194 changed the situation overnight. There was an immediate revival of interest on the part of the Technical Department of the Air Ministry in the rocket-driven interceptor concept, and as the Me 163 airframes under construction at Augsburg-Haunstetten were intended to prove the practicability of rocket propulsion for aircraft, rather than its military potentialities, Lippisch was ordered to give the highest priority to the development of a fully-operational interceptor version of the Me 163. Simultaneously, the number of prototypes of the initial model was increased from two to six, this first version becoming the Me 163A and the projected interceptor variant being assigned the designation Me 163B.

The importance now attached to the Me 163 development programme resulted in immediate acceleration of prototype construction, and the first prototype airframe had been completed at Lechfeld, to where the manufacturing programme had been transferred, before the end of 1940. Hellmuth Walter was by this time testing an improved rocket motor, the HWK R II-203b, which,like the R I-203 that had, powered the He 176,used T-Stoff and, Z-Stoff but had circulatory pumps for both liquids, and offered a thrust of 1,650 pounds. Lippisch elected to install the R II-203b in the Me 163A, but prior to powered trials the handling characteristics of the radical little airplane had to be explored thoroughly in gliding flight, and tests began at Lechfeld in the early spring of 1941 with the first prototype, the Me 163A V1 (Versuchs-Eins or Experimental One).

Heini Dittmar was again the test pilot, and a Bf 110C fighter was used to tow the Me 163A V1 into the air. From the outset the prototype revealed an exceptionally flat gliding angle, sinking speed being only five feet per second at 137mph, but Dittmar quickly discovered that, owing to its tendency to float and its lack of flaps, the aircraft was extremely difficult to put down within the boundaries of the airfield, and it floated several hundred yards past Dittmar's intended point of touchdown and sailed over the boundary hedge into an adjacent field. Fortunately, the prototype suffered no damage, and it was decided to tow it to the larger airfield at Augsburg-Haunstetten, but the ferry flight nearly ended in the loss of the aircraft. After casting off from the towplane, Dittmar made a leisurely circuit of the field and then began his approach, but soon realised that he had misjudged the sink and was going to overshoot the field with little chance of missing some temporary drainage ditches that had been dug on the far side of the boundary. In desperation, Dittmar banked the aircraft violently, just succeeded in slipping through a narrow gap between two hangars, and landed crosswind.

Gliding trials from Augsburg-Haunstetten revealed a glide angle of 1:20 despite the fact that the aircraft possessed an aspect ratio of only 1:4.4. Severe rudder flutter was experienced at 225mph, and at 325mph aileron flutter manifested itself, but correct balancing eradicated these troubles, and the general flying characteristics of the Me 163A V1 proved to be extraordinarily good. Ernst Udet witnessed one of the high-speed gliding trials of the aircraft during a visit to Augsburg-Haunstetten, arriving just as Dittmar cast off from his towplane at 16,000 feet and began his test programme. Udet joined Alexander Lippisch, pointed to the boomerang-like shape wheeling above, and said, 'What in heaven's name is that, Lippisch?' Lippisch replied that it was the Me 163, just as Dittmar, who had put the aircraft into a steep dive, flashed past at over 400mph with no more sound than a subdued whistle, and then soared upwards. 'What sort of engine has it?' enquired Udet. With some amusement, Lippisch replied, 'None!' Nonplussed, Udet watched Dittmar flash down again from above, glide around the field several times to use up his excess speed, and then start his landing approach.

'No engine! Impossible!' grunted Udet, and hurried across the field to where the odd-looking aircraft had now come to a standstill. He walked round the Me 163, muttering, 'My God! It's true – it has no engine!' Dittmar explained that it would eventually receive a rocket motor,

and although Udet had refused to listen to any proposals concerning rocket propulsion for aircraft since what he referred to as the 'He 176 fiasco', he had been so impressed by Dittmar's performance that he promised Lippisch his whole-hearted support in developing the Me 163, subsequently proving as good as his word and intervening on behalf of the aircraft on two occasions when the Technical Department proposed that its priority should be reduced.

During the summer of 1941, by which time several other A-series prototype airframes had been completed, the first and fourth aircraft, the Me 163A V1 and V4, were transferred to Peenemünde for installation of their R II-203 b rocket motors, and the first 'sharp start' was performed by Heini Dittmar in July. During the earliest of these trials Dittmar experienced no difficulty in exceeding the existing world air speed record, and was soon attaining speeds of the order of 500 mph and then 550mph, the speeds being

Lippisch's DFS 194 (above), coupled with the piloting expertise of Heinrich 'Heini' Dittmar (right), were to result in Messerschmitt's Komet

measured on the ground by a battery of Askania kinetheodolites. The Me 163 undoubtedly possessed excellent flying characteristics, but take-off presented serious problems, as it took place from a narrow-track, unsprung two-wheel dolly, the only cushioning effect being provided by its small rubber tyres. Without some form of shock absorber, a successful take-off from this dolly, which was jettisoned once the aircraft was airborne, was by no means assured. The aircraft had to be kept straight and level on the dolly until unstick speed of about 125 mph was attained. All take-offs had to be made directly into wind, and if the wind veered a change in the direction of take-off was necessary, and the surface of the field ahead of the aircraft had to be examined with extreme care as uneven ground could result

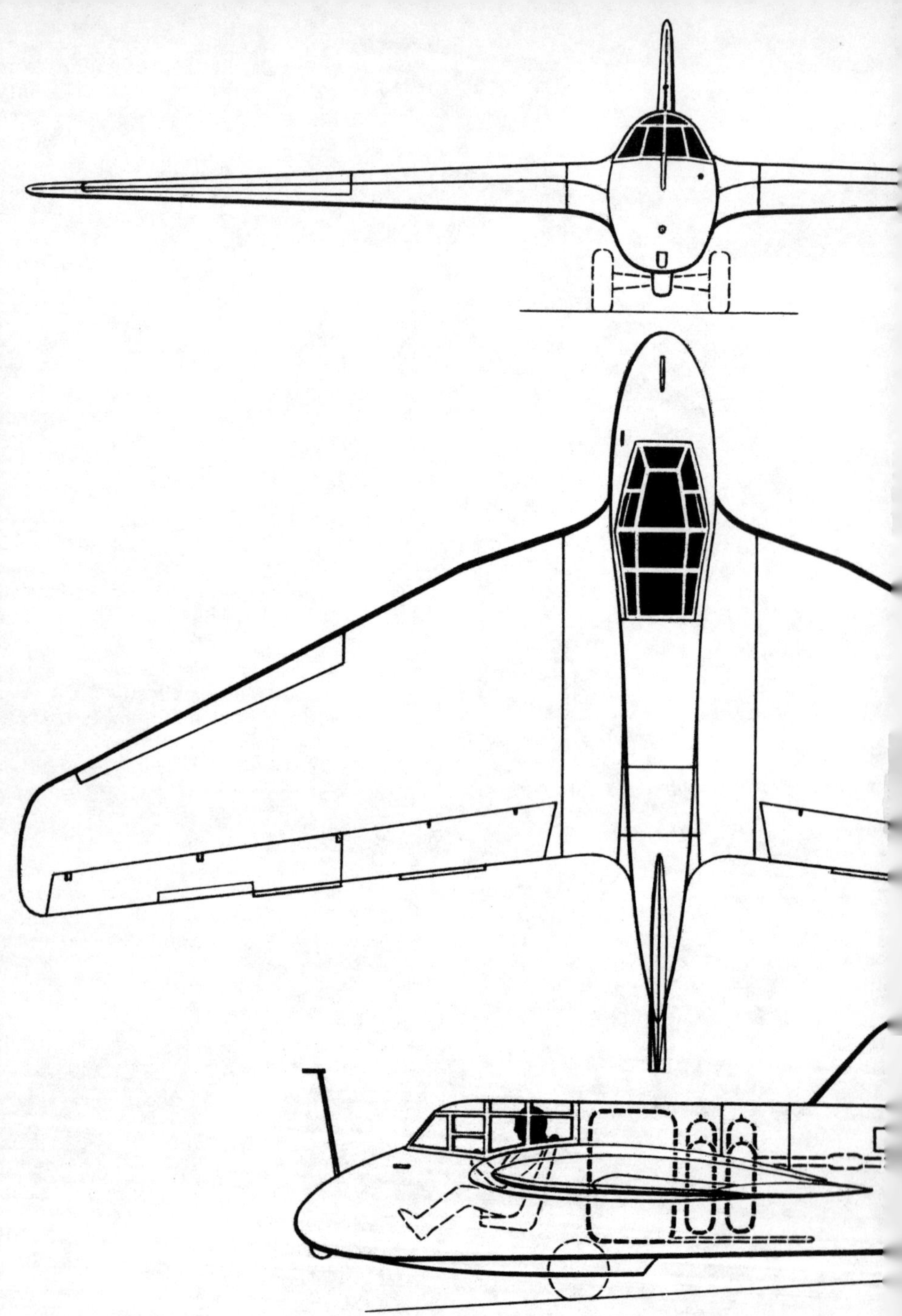

The bat-like DFS 194. It was never intended for rocket power, but was modified to take a Walter motor both to accelerate the test programme and to revive flagging official interest in the potentialities of rocket propulsion for manned aircraft

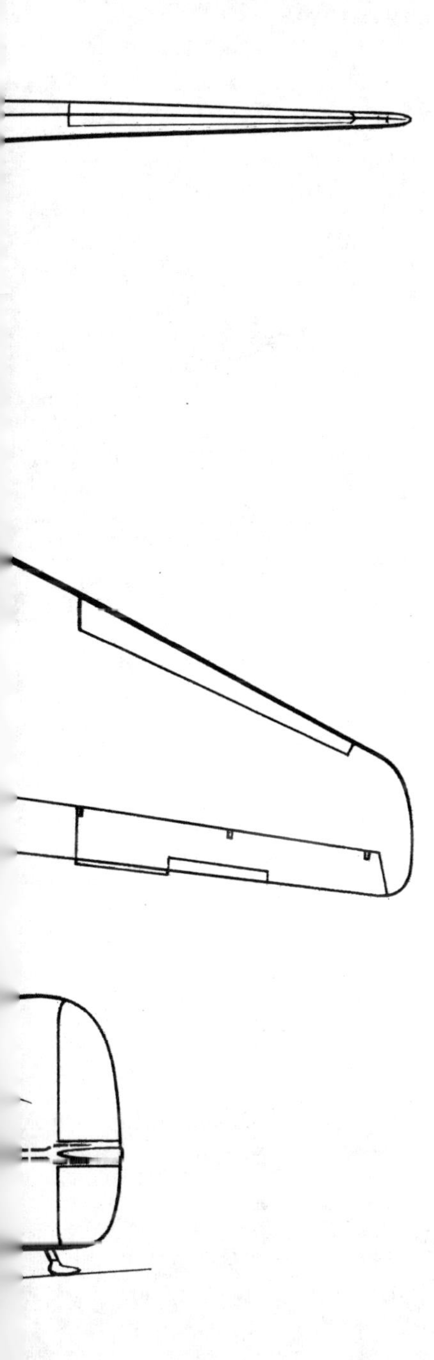

in premature unstick. Take-off from a concrete runway could be made only with a strong headwind blowing from exactly the right direction. During a calm or with a crosswind take-off was impossible as the aircraft simply veered off course because the rudder had no effect until a certain minimum speed had been achieved. This shortcoming was eventually to lead to the development of the so-called Strahlruder (jet rudder) which provided a measure of control from the moment the rocket motor was ignited.

The Me 163A weighed 3,197 pounds in empty equipped condition, and with 140 US gallons of T-Stoff and Z-Stoff, when fully tanked up it weighed 5,291 pounds. Calculations indicated that the Me 163 was capable of still higher speeds than those attained during the initial test phase, but their attainment revolved around the fuel capacity of the aircraft which was only sufficient for four-and-a-half minutes of powered flight. This set a limitation of about 570mph on the speed that could be reached. On 2nd October 1941, Dittmar had the Me 163A V4 fully tanked up and, in order to conserve fuel, towed to an altitude of 13,120 feet behind a Bf 110C fighter. After casting off from the towplane and firing the rocket motor, Dittmar had accelerated to 624mph, or about Mach 0.84, when compressibility effects resulted in a sudden loss of stability, and the aircraft went into a dive. Dittmar promptly cut the rocket, and the aircraft decelerated rapidly until full control was restored.

Details of the flight were immediately evaluated and forwarded to the Air Ministry in Berlin that same evening, but most officials refused to believe that such a speed could have been achieved, and Dr Göthert, the Director of the DVL (German Aviation Experimental Establishment) was hurriedly sent to Peenemünde to check the measured performance figures and compare them with calculated values obtained at Göttingen. Dr Göthert was

The first of two prototypes initiated as Project X, the Me 163A V1 is seen above at Augsburg-Haunstetten, and below making a 'sharp start' at Peenemünde

The Me 163A V1, seen above and below in gliding flight, possessed extraordinarily good flying characteristics, which were retained by the Komet

seriously disgruntled when forced to confirm the accuracy of the figures; his tunnel at the DVL was only capable of measuring speeds up to Mach 0.8 but there was no denying that Dittmar had flown at a speed substantially in excess of this. Ernst Udet, temporarily emerging from the depression that was to end in his suicide a few weeks later, was suddenly 'all fire and flames', as Alexander Lippisch subsequently related, demanding that weapons be mounted in 'this fantastic airplane' immediately. Lippisch patiently explained the impracticability of installing armament in the existing aircraft, adding that such would be senseless in any case as construction of the more advanced Me 163B was scheduled to commence on 1st December, and this model had been designed from the outset as a combat airplane. Dittmar was later to receive the Lilienthal Award for Aeronautical Research for this epoch-marking flight.

It was ascertained that the sudden change in pitch stability that had sent the Me 163A V4 plunging into an uncontrollable dive had resulted from the retention of a wing essentially similar to that of the DFS 194 which had a considerable wash-out, the wingtips having a compressibility stall in the negative lift range. By comparison with that of the DFS 194, the wing of the Me 163A, which had a span of 30ft 7¼in, was swept twenty degrees on the inboard leading edge and thirty-two degrees outboard (the respective sweep angles of the DFS 194 being nineteen and twenty-seven degrees) and featured six degrees less trailing-edge sweep. Lippisch concluded, therefore, that the wing planform of the Me 163B should be revised, a constant 23.3 degrees of sweepback being adopted at quarter-chord, and to safeguard against wingtip stall, special low-drag fixed slots, known as C-slots and devised by a member of Lippisch's team, J Hubert, were applied to the outboard forty per cent of the wing, immediately in front of the elevons. These slots presented a drag penalty of only 2.5 per cent of the entire aircraft, and rendered the Me 163 incapable of spinning; with crossed controls the aircraft merely side-slipped.

To all intents and purposes, the combat version of the Me 163 was a complete redesign, retaining no more than the basic configuration of the original model, and construction of six prototypes began on 1st December 1941. The first of these left the assembly line during the following April, but while Lippisch's fighter was ready Walter's power plant was not. This – the HWK R II-211 – was a derivative of the Walter HWK 501 take-off assistance rocket which afforded a thrust of 3,310 pounds for thirty seconds and had been ordered into production to aid overloaded He 111 and Ju 88 bombers. The HWK 501 differed from earlier Walter rockets in being of the 'hot' type, a bi-propellant in which a second fuel was introduced to burn with the decomposition products of the T-Stoff. This catalyst was known as C-Stoff, a thirty per cent hydrazine hydrate solution in methanol, which, combined with T-Stoff, possessed frightening volatility. Walter introduced means of varying the thrust for the R II-211 intended for the Me 163B; a 120hp steam turbine was added to drive the fuel pumps, and to solve the problem of cooling, the fuel was first circulated into a cooling jacket before being injected into the combustion chamber.

It was calculated that, at full thrust, the R II-211 would consume approximately six pounds of T-Stoff per second, and on the basis of this calculation, Lippisch and his team had been asked to provide tankage sufficient for twelve minutes' flight at full thrust. It was estimated that the Me 163B would require some three minutes' full thrust to reach an altitude of 39,370 feet at which point thrust could be reduced to translate the remaining nine minutes of full power into some thirty minutes of horizontal flight at about 590mph, tactical radius thus being of the order of 150 miles. Unfortunately, at the time these calculations were made the R II-211 rocket motor existed only in mock-up form, and when the Me 163B V1 was rolled out in April 1942, three running tests of the power plant had all terminated abruptly in the R II-211 blowing up. More than a year was to elapse before Hellmuth Walter's 'hot' rocket was to be cleared for flight testing, and even then it was still to be considered very much an 'experimental' power plant. Bench tests had forced the propulsion experts to admit that its fuel consumption was almost double that previously calculated (T-Stoff consumption rate being eleven pounds per second at maximum thrust) and thus the Me 163B tankage was barely sufficient for six minutes at full throttle.

An order had meanwhile been placed with Messerschmitt's plant at Regensburg for no fewer than seventy pre-production Me 163B airframes. The remaining B-series prototype airframes had left the assembly line at short intervals, and Heini Dittmar had been joined in the Me 163 flight development programme at Peenemünde by Rudolf 'Pitz' Opitz. Like Dittmar, Opitz had been a test pilot at the German Research Institute for Gliding Flight (DFS) at Darmstadt-Griesheim. In 1939 he had been called up for service with the highly secret glider-borne air-landing commando which was to provide the nucleus of the Luftlandegeschwader 1, the Luftwaffe's first 'Air-landing Group' and the first unit of its kind in the world. After participating in the audacious glider assault of 10th May 1940, which had resulted in the capture of the Eben-Emael fortifications and the Kanne, Veldwezelt and Vroenhoven bridges, 'Pitz' Opitz had been assigned as an instructor to a newly-created school for assault and transport glider pilots – the school which eventually became the Fliegerschule 4 für Lastensegler. In the early autumn

Rudolf 'Pitz' Opitz joined the Me 163 programme at Peenemünde in 1942

of 1941, Lippisch had requested that Opitz be released from his Luftwaffe assignment so that he could join Dittmar at Peenemünde, and, with the aid of Ernst Udet, has succeeded in obtaining his services.

During the summer months of 1942, Dittmar and Opitz put the prototypes of the Me 163B through every test that could be conducted with the airplane in its unpowered form, including gun-firing trials. The flying characteristics of the Me 163B proved superb even when flown up to maximum weight (provided by water ballast). The degree of control was outstanding, and despite its tailless configuration, Lippisch's fighter was stable about all axes. During this flight test phase, Opitz flew one of the Me 163B prototypes which had been equipped with a drogue parachute designed to decelerate the aircraft in an emergency, thus enabling the pilot to bale out using the Luftwaffe's standard parachute that was considered unsafe at a speed of more than 280mph. During the first test with this device, the Me 163B was towed to 16,400 feet behind a Bf 110C fighter. Opitz then cast off from the towplane and dived until the aircraft was travelling at some 500mph and was down to an

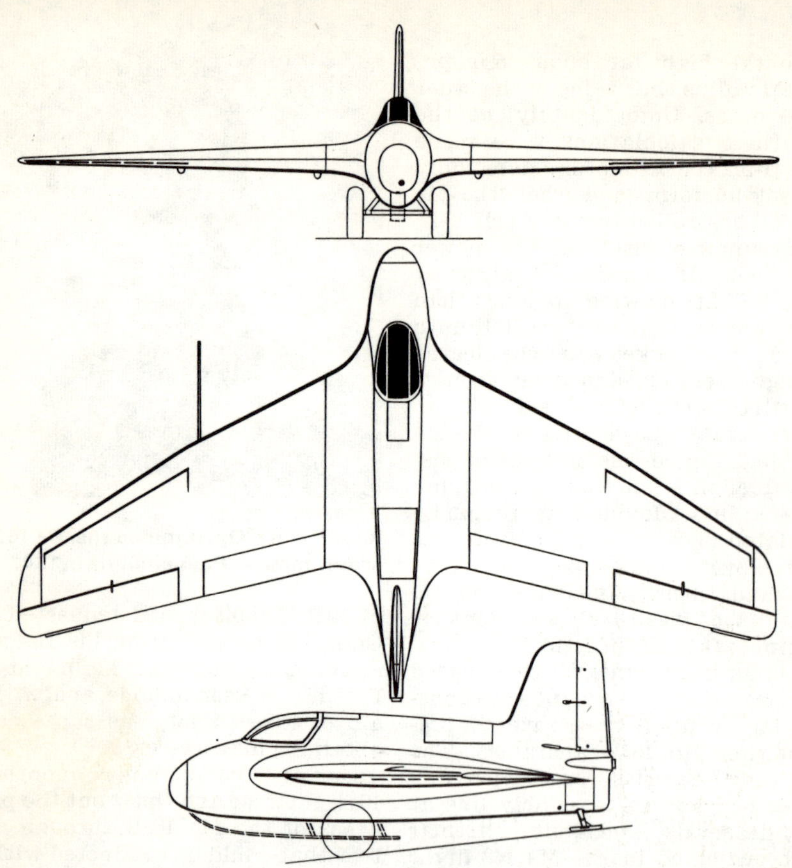

The Messerschmitt Me 163A. Although possessing a close affinity with the DFS 194, this design bore little similarity to the Me 163B Komet apart from general configuration. The few Me 163As built were used for training Komet pilots

altitude of 8,200 feet. He then levelled out and deployed the tail-mounted braking parachute.

After measuring the deceleration, Opitz attempted to jettison the parachute, but the release mechanism refused to function. Baling out threatened to foul the braking parachute, and his only alternative was to attempt a landing with the parachute fully deployed. Once more putting the aircraft into a dive to build up as much speed as the drag of the parachute allowed, Optiz levelled off over the airfield boundary, and tried to coax the Me 163B to settle. Despite the braking effect of the trailing parachute the airplane persisted in remaining airborne, floated across the field, and finally came to rest on the other side of the far boundary in a turnip field.

The test programme encountered a major setback late in 1942 as a result of serious injuries suffered by Heini Dittmar. The Me 163B was fitted with a retractable skid which was lowered hydraulically for landing, and embodied a shock-absorbing oleo leg. Dittmar was demonstrating the effect of improved landing flaps, and had planned to land immediately in front of a hangar where Alexander Lippisch and several of his technicians were assembled; but as he approached the touchdown point with skid extended, he inadvertently glided into the windless space behind the hangar.

Stalling from a height of about twelve feet, he hit the concrete apron with considerable force. Unfortunately for Dittmar, the prototype that he was flying had just been fitted with a modified seat permitting little flexibility of movement; the oleo leg of the skid had absorbed only a small proportion of the impact, and most of the force had been transmitted directly to Dittmar's body. His spinal chord was badly damaged and the injuries that it had sustained were to necessitate a two-year sojourn in hospital.

The rocket people at Kiel were optimistic as to the availability of the HWK R II-211 motor for the Me 163B. Weeks had become months, and the so-called 'hot' engine still refused to function with any degree of reliability. The fuel feed lines frequently malfunctioned, the 'pot' or combustion chamber often blew itself up, and the handling of the fuels, with their highly explosive properties, was proving hazardous in the extreme. Both T-Stoff and C-Stoff were colorless fluids, and on one occasion an unfortunate mechanic poured a few pints of the latter into a bucket containing a minute quantity of the former. Before he realised the magnitude of his mistake his remains had been spread thinly over the entire test shed. The greatest caution had to be exercised in sealing all T-Stoff containers as even a tiny insect or a few dust particles could set off a chain reaction with disastrous results, while the C-Stoff corroded anything other than a glass, enamel or anodically-treated container.

Under other circumstances there can be little doubt that the entire project would have been 'put on ice' pending a thorough-going reappraisal of the power plant and its fuels, but preparations had already been made for the quantity production of the Me 163B on the strength of the outstanding initial test results. Materials had been stockpiled, jigs had been constructed and, by early 1943, the first pre-production airframes were, in fact, rolling off the Regensburg assembly line. Furthermore, the first vestiges of a sense of urgency had begun to manifest themselves.

For several months following Dittmar's accident, Opitz was forced to carry the entire burden of the Me 163B flight test programme. Early in 1943, however, Hauptmann Wolfgang Späte, who had been appointed Luftwaffe liaison officer to the Me 163 programme, arrived at Peenemünde from Rechlin with the primary task of forming a development and tactical evaluation unit, the Erprobungskommando (Test Detachment) 16, or EK 16.

Späte was a highly experienced sailplane pilot who, after serving with an army co-operation and tactical reconnaissance unit during the offensive in the west, had transferred to the fighter arm, joining the 5th Staffel of Jagdgeschwader 54 on 1st January 1941. Flying Messerschmitt Bf 109s in the Balkans and over the Soviet Union, Späte, who had been appointed Staffekapitän in the autumn of 1941, had soon proved himself an outstanding fighter pilot. He was awarded the Knight's Cross of the Iron Cross on 5th October 1941, and the highly-coveted Oak Leaves to the Knight's Cross on 23rd April 1942, by which time he had been responsible for no fewer than seventy-two confirmed 'kills'. Späte was quickly joined at Peenemünde by four other 'old glider hands': Hauptmann Anthony 'Toni' Thaler, a veteran flying instructor and former ferry pilot, Oberleutnant Josef 'Joschi' Pöhs from Jagdgeschwader 54 and Oberleutnant Johannes Kiel from Zerstörergeschwader 26, both holders of the Knight's Cross, and Second Lieutenant Herber Langer, a veteran of Jagdgeschwader 53. These provided the pilot nucleus of EK 16 which immediately commenced training on the Me 163A, the prototypes of this initial model having been augmented by a further ten airframes built by the Wolf Hirth works at Nabern.

From an early stage in their relationship, a strong conflict of personalities had been apparent between Alexander Lippisch and Willy Messerschmitt. The Me 163 had not been fathered on Messerschmitt's drawing boards and with the arrival of the Project X team at Augsburg-Haunstetten his rôle had become increasingly that of an unwilling foster parent. Messerschmitt had soon begun to display total disinterest in Lippisch's work; relations between the two designers had steadily deteriorated until, by early 1943, Lippisch considered them insupportable, and, on 1st May, left the Messerschmitt organisation to take up an appointment as Director of the Vienna Aviation Research Establishment. His departure hardly augured well for the future of his rocket-propelled interceptor.

In July 1943, the first flight-cleared HWK R II-211 rocket motors arrived at Peenemünde. They were still far from reliable but some fifteen months had elapsed since the completion of the first prototype Me 163B airframe. Further delay could not be countenanced – irrespective of the consequences. All but a few of the seventy pre-production airplanes had by now left the Regensburg assembly line, and the Klemm Technik GmbH (an offshoot of the well-known lightplane manufacturing concern of Klemm-Flugzeugbau GmbH of Böblingen) had already been assigned the task of supervising series production. The overall plan was to produce components in factories in various parts of Germany and assemble them in a highly secret plant situated in the Black Forest. More than half the Regensburg-built pre-production airplanes had been assigned Versuchs (Experimental) numbers, those not allocated such numbers being given the designation Me 163Ba-1 and the task of service evaluation.

The rocket motor was mounted in several B-series airframes simultaneously early in July, the first installation completed being in the Me 163B V2. After a series of ground runs with the prototype anchored rigidly to a test rig, Opitz considered the rocket motor to have displayed sufficient reliability for flight testing to be warranted. In the event, the initial powered flight test very nearly ended in disaster before the airplane had left the ground. During the take-off run the twin-wheel dolly separated from the Me 163 before flying speed had been attained, and the aircraft shot forward on its landing skid. Fortunately for Opitz, in view of the powder-keg potentialities of his partly tanked-up prototype, he succeeded in pulling it off the ground before it reached the airfield boundary, but his troubles were by no means over. As he began his climb-out, the cockpit filled with T-Stoff steam, forcing him to activate the canopy-jettisoning mechanism. Half-blinded, he succeeded in making a circuit of the field, by which time his vision had recovered sufficiently for him to make a safe landing. In this somewhat hesitant fashion, the Komet, as the Me 163B was to become known, was at last born. Its gestation had been lengthy, and teething was to prove a painful process, as Opitz was all too soon to discover.

A few days later, on 20th July, Opitz attempted to fly the Me 163B V21 with virtually full tanks. The weight of the airplane at take-off was 7,061 pounds, this including 2,293 pounds of T-Stoff and 750 pounds of C-Stoff. According to the flight test report subsequently filed by Opitz, take-off was completed without difficulty despite a seventy-degree sidewind of 9mph, and was followed by a normal climb at full thrust. At an altitude of some 26,250 feet Opitz began to experience violent thrust variations from the rocket motor. The fluctuating thrust was accompanied by a flashing fire warning light, and at 27,890 feet Opitz cut the

The difference between the Me 163A and the Me 163B Komet interceptor (with dappled camouflage) is clearly shown by these photos

The Me 163B V21, a pre-series test aircraft used at Peenemünde

rocket. Gliding to a lower altitude he attempted to re-ignite the power plant without success but managed to effect a good landing. It was then discovered that 287 pounds of fuel remained in the tanks, and the power plant was promptly removed for examination and bench running trials in an attempt to ascertain the reasons for the fluctuating thrust and the refusal of the motor to re-ignite. Some time was to pass, however, before answers were to be found, and meanwhile a heavy Allied bombing attack on Peenemünde necessitated the transfer of EK 16 to an airfield less likely to suffer the attentions of the enemy.

The new site selected for the Me 163 programme was an airfield near Bad Zwischenahn, in Oldenburg. During the hurried transfer from Peenemünde, Opitz was ordered to ferry an Me 163B with malfunctioning landing flap hydraulics to Bad Zwischenahn. After dropping his towline over the new base, Opitz began his approach but quickly discovered that the landing skid would not extend. He had no alternative but to land on the retracted skid, seriously damaging his spinal chord in the process. The injury necessitated three months in hospital, and, if less extensive, was so similar to that suffered by Dittmar during the previous year that Dr Justus Schneider, a specialist in the field of aviation medicine, was called in to advise on means of overcoming such accidents.

It was calculated that an impact force equivalent to some twenty times that of gravity had been sustained by Dittmar and Opitz, and it was technically impossible to construct a landing skid capable of absorbing impact stresses of such magnitude. Dr Schneider proposed a torsion-sprung seat that would at least cushion the critical stresses, and the seat design which evolved as a result of this proposal was eventually adopted as standard for the series production Me 163B.

At the time of its arrival at Bad Zwischenahn, the Komet, if past infancy, was still far from maturity. The pilots of EK 16 had to become experts in precision landing, touching down as closely as possible to a cross marked on the runway. If the pilot failed to touch down within a reasonable distance of the cross and skidded onto rough ground, the chances were that the airplane would turn turtle and the highly temperamental rocket fuels remaining in its tanks would explode. Pilots assigned to EK 16 normally underwent some training on the so-called Stummel-Habicht, a slipped-wing version of the Habicht (Hawk) glider, at Gelnhausen before being introduced to the Me 163A. The training syllabus normally comprised six towed take-offs with empty and water-ballastedMe 163As, two 'sharp starts' or powered take-offs, one half-endurance powered flight, and two full-endurance powered flights before conversion to the Me 163B on which the sequence was repeated.

Some trouble was experienced by EK 16 with rocket motors cutting out for no apparent reason. Sometimes at the most critical point of flight – shortly after take-off when the aircraft was just over the airfield boundary with tanks three-quarters full and airspeed at about 240mph – the rocket motor would flame out. One pilot had to make an emergency landing with virtually full tanks, two aircraft crashed, and several pilots escaped injury by a hair's breadth. The problem did not reveal itself during bench running as it was impossible to simulate the acceleration condition. However, it was eventually discovered that there was a build-up of turbulence in the fuel outlet which, under certain conditions, sucked air in and shut off the fuel control unit. This problem was eventually overcome by the introduction of vertical baffles above the outlet.

The casualties of the Komet programme began to mount at Bad Zwischenahn, but before the arrival of Lippisch's fighter at this field, the Komet claimed several victims apart from Heini Dittmar. Perhaps the most distinguished of these was Hanna Reitsch, the first woman pilot to have received the honorary title of Flugkapitän which had been bestowed on her by Ernst Udet in 1937 after she had given a remarkable demonstration at Darmstadt-Griesheim of the capabilities of newly-developed air brakes.

Together with Opitz and Späte, Hanna Reitsch had been assigned the task of performing the flight acceptance tests of the unpowered pre-production Me 163Bs as they left the Regensburg assembly line. The tests were flown from Obertraubling, the newly-completed aircraft being towed into the air behind a Messerschmitt Bf 110. The first four acceptance flights performed by Hanna Reitsch were uneventful but the fifth had ended in catastrophe.

At an altitude of thirty feet she had attempted to jettison the undercarriage dolly, but the release lever had not activated the jettisoning mechanism, and as speed increased the aircraft had begun to vibrate violently. Hanna Reitsch was unaware of the cause of the vibration until she saw the observer in the rear cockpit of the towplane waving violently and its pilot lowering and raising his undercarriage. Anxious to reach an altitude at which she could safely drop the towline and discover if the Komet would answer to the controls despite the drag and weight of the take-off dolly, she had eventually succeeded in making the Bf 110 pilot understand her plan, and had been towed slowly to an altitude of 10,500 feet. At this point she had cast off the tow. But every effort to dislodge the dolly had proved abortive, and the aircraft had continued to vibrate strongly. Eventually it had answered to control movements – if somewhat sluggishly – and Hanna Reitsch had

Above and *below*: Tanking up one of the test Komets, the Me 163B V28, with T-Stoff at Bad Zwischenahn in preparation for a 'sharp start'

Above: Steam is vented from an Me 163Ba-1. *Below:* Water is passed under pressure through the steam generator during functional tests

Above: The Walter 509A rocket motor on a test stand at Bad Zwischenahn. *Below:* An Me 163Ba-1 with the rear fuselage detached

Above: The skid of the Komet extended in landing position. *Below:* The jettisonable take-off dolly is attached to the skid

Right: **A Komet makes a 'sharp start' with take-off dolly still attached.**
Below right: **The dolly is jettisoned**

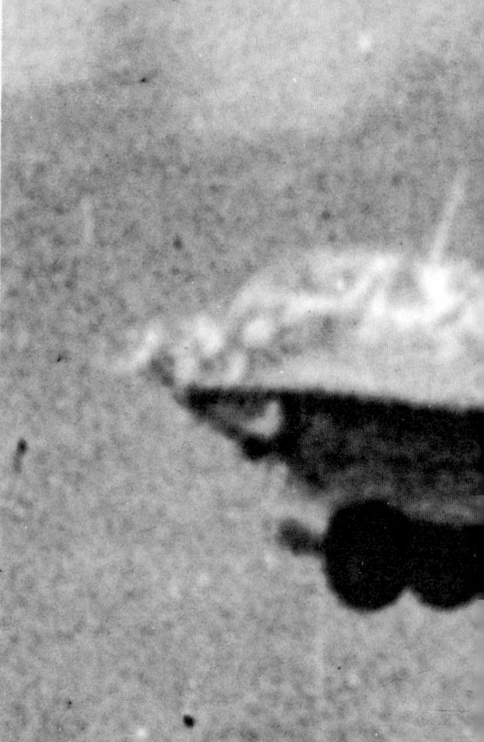

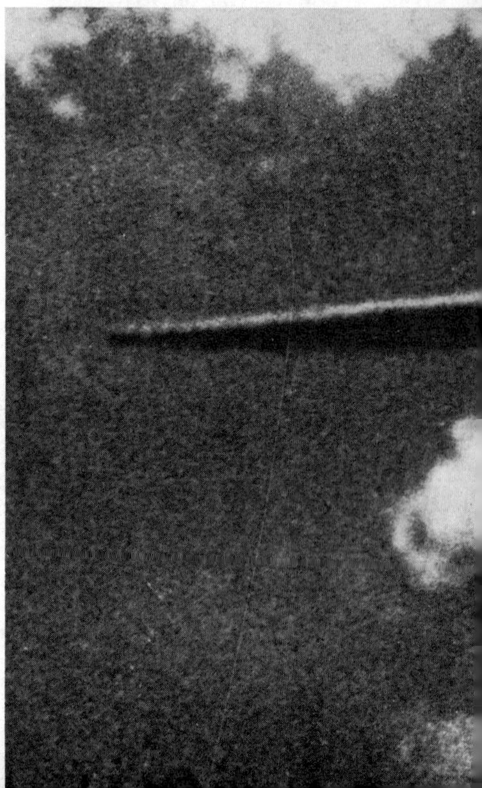

decided to attempt a landing. Her idea was to make a high approach and then, during the last hundred yards, sideslip the aircraft down to the edge of the field. Unfortunately, owing to the turbulence set up by the undercarriage dolly, the controls had become ineffective the moment the aircraft began side-slipping and she had stalled in from about a hundred feet, the aircraft hitting the ground with tremendous force. In this accident Hanna Reitsch had suffered six fractures of the skull and displacement of the upper jawbone.

The appalling hazards of flying the Komet at this stage in its development were later to be portrayed graphically by a new recruit to EK 16, Leutnant Mano Ziegler, in his account of the demise of a fellow pupil, Feldwebel Alois Wörndl, during the first powered take-offs of the Me 163B at Bad Zwischenahn: ' A certain Feldwebel Alois Wörndl from Aschau, an excellent fellow and completely reliable, flying with the accuracy of a precision instrument, was chosen from among us pupils to make the first sharp start in the Komet. "Make it good, Alois!" we shouted, and then he was off. To make our first sharp take-offs in the Komet less dangerous the fuel tanks were not filled to the brim, although, in our opinion, a few hundred litres one way or another did not much affect the odds – it was still T-Stoff! Of course, this meant that the Komet could not get up to its full operational altitude and remained within our sight throughout the test.'

'As expected, Alois's rocket motor cut at about 6,000 metres altitude, and he turned back towards the field, gliding down according to instructions, as precise as ever. We could see the Komet flattening out preparatory to landing, and then, without warning, "Sideslip!" The shout came from one of the group. We could now all see

Left: **A test Komet lands at Bad Zwischenahn, the starboard wing dipping (in lower photo) as momentum is lost**

only too clearly that Alois was much too high to touch down anywhere near the landing cross! "Sideslip, sideslip!" we all shouted as if he could hear us, but the Komet shot past us and past the landing cross – too high, too fast! We watched with horror as it floated away across the airfield as though some invisible hand was holding the aircraft away from the safety of the runway. Anxiously we watched the Komet touch down far outside the airfield perimeter, rebound into the air, drop back again like a brick, and then skid into some rough ground and turn over on its back. A split-second later a blinding white flame shot up, followed by a mushroom of smoke'.

Shortly before Wörndl's accident, EK 16 had lost Oberleutnant Josef Pöhs, one of the first of the Luftwaffe pilots to join the Me 163 programme at Peenemünde, and Technical Officer of the Test Detachment after its arrival at Bad Zwischenahn. On the morning of 30th December 1943, Pöhs had made a 'sharp start' in one of the Me 163As, but the heavy steel undercarriage dolly had rebounded from the ground and hit the aircraft. Pöhs had succeeded in retaining control, but the dolly had evidently fractured a T-Stoff feedline. The aircraft shot up to 300 feet, banked steeply back towards the field, and had then dropped like a stone, hitting the ground at an angle. It had skidded along the runway crabwise for some fifty yards before coming to a standstill, but by the time the ambulance and fire tender had reached the aircraft Pöhs was dead. He had presumably been knocked unconscious on impact and had then been literally dissolved alive by the T-Stoff that has seeped into the cockpit from the fractured feedline.

Advanced concept - abysmal failure

While totally unaware of Soviet work in the field of rocket-propelled interceptors, US and British Intelligence was not entirely ignorant of the radical trend taken by fighter development in Germany, and work had in fact begun in the USA on the development of a rocket-driven interceptor of even more advanced concept than the Komet – a radical flying wing in which the pilot lay prone. This work had stemmed from a proposal made to the USAAF Air Material Command in September 1942 by John K Northrop, President and Chief Engineer of Northrop Aircraft Incorporated and a man of remarkable inventive ability and original ideas.

At the time that John Northrop had presented the AAF with his proposals, rocket motor development in the USA was very much in its infancy, and service interest had been largely confined to the application of rockets as take-off-assistance devices. The AAF had begun work on JATO (Jet-Assisted Take-Off) units in 1939 through the Guggenheim Aeronautical Laboratory of the California Institute of Technology. The programme called for the development of long-burning solid-propellant rockets and larger liquid-propellant rockets based on the use of any oxidant other than liquid oxygen which was considered impracticable for field use by the AAF. The first result was a solid-propellant motor providing twenty-eight pounds of thrust for twelve seconds on a two-pound charge of GALCIT-27, an amide powder, and this motor was tested successfully beneath an Ercoupe light plane in August 1941. Flown by Homer A Boushey, the Ercoupe was fitted with two three-unit rocket clusters beneath each wing which cut take-off time and distance by some fifty per cent. A total of 152 firings were completed without a single failure, and Boushey reported that, if anything, the JATO units actually improved controllability.

Simultaneously work being carried out on a liquid-propellant rocket offering about 1,800 pounds of thrust was rewarded with success on 4th July 1940 when a satisfactory trial run was completed after three earlier test motors had exploded. The motor used gasoline and nitric acid, but this highly volatile combination had given trouble at the Annapolis Naval Air Station (where work on liquid-propellant JATO units was also being undertaken) and the suggestion was made that aniline – hypergolic with nitric acid – be introduced as a gasoline additive. The next stage was the replacement of the gasoline by aniline as fuel, and reliability was so improved that an acid-aniline motor was mounted in the rear of the port engine nacelle of a Douglas A-20 bomber, and successfully tested in flight in April 1942 by Colonel Paul Dane. At this stage, the project was turned over to the Aerojet Corporation which was assigned the task of designing and manufacturing the production unit.

It had been the successful development of the liquid-propellant JATO unit that had inspired John Northrop to consider the possibilities of a rocket-propelled interceptor, and the AAF agreed that such an airplane possessed considerable potential – promising high speed, a phenominal climb rate and an outstanding operational ceiling. Aerojet had already begun work on acid-aniline rocket motors capable of substantially longer burning times than those required for JATO tasks, capable of being re-ignited an almost unlimited number of times in the air, and offering thrust regulation. John Northrop believed that such a power plant capable of giving some 2,000 pounds of thrust would be ideally suited to the airplane he had in mind – an airplane in which the physical dimensions of the human frame were the limiting size factor, and for which reason a prone position was desirable for the pilot. Such pilot accommodation allowed the cockpit to be no more than a slight thickening of the wing section, would result in the presentation of the minimum silhouette to enemy gunners, and, it was believed, enable the pilot to withstand plus twelve-g acceleration and reduce the strain imposed by violent manoeuvres and sudden pull-outs.

Northrop proposed that the primary structural material should be heavy welded magnesium plate. He appreciated the fact that red fuming nitric used by the Aerojet rocket motor as an oxidant had a highly corrosive effect on magnesium (whereas stainless steel and aluminum remained unaffected) but considered that the protection of the integral fuel tanks from battle damage was of primary importance; any mixing of the acid and aniline other than in the combustion chamber, which might occur as a result of tank damage, would almost inevitably result in the loss of the aircraft. Heavy gauge magnesium offered the best possible protection for the tanks, and the development of an effective protective coating to prevent the acid coming into contact with the magnesium structure did not appear to present an insurmountable problem.

The prone pilot position and the extensive use of magnesium in the structure of the aircraft were radical enough features, but no more so than the flying wing configuration. John Northrop had been devoting his attention to the design of aircraft of the 'flying wing' type since the early 1920s. His first aircraft to be dubbed a 'flying wing', built in 1928 at Burbank, California, had not in fact been a true 'flying wing' as insufficient aerodynamic data was then available to its designer to ensure the airplane's stability without a tail. It had therefore been fitted with an orthodox empennage carried by tubular booms, but it did feature the immensely thick wing centre section and radical degree of taper that were to characterise the later Northrop designs of genuine flying wing form.

The AAF was already sold on the flying wing configuration, having ordered four N9M one-third flying scale models of the XB-35 four-engined heavy bomber of which prototypes had also been contracted for. But Northrop Aircraft was too heavily committed to take on yet another major development programme: it lacked sufficient engineering manpower and shop facilities. The AAF therefore agreed to accept John Northrop's rocket-powered interceptor project, but only on the understanding that Northrop Aircraft subcontracted one hundred per cent of the engineering and fabrication, retaining responsibility for only the general supervision of the project.

In January 1943, procurement of

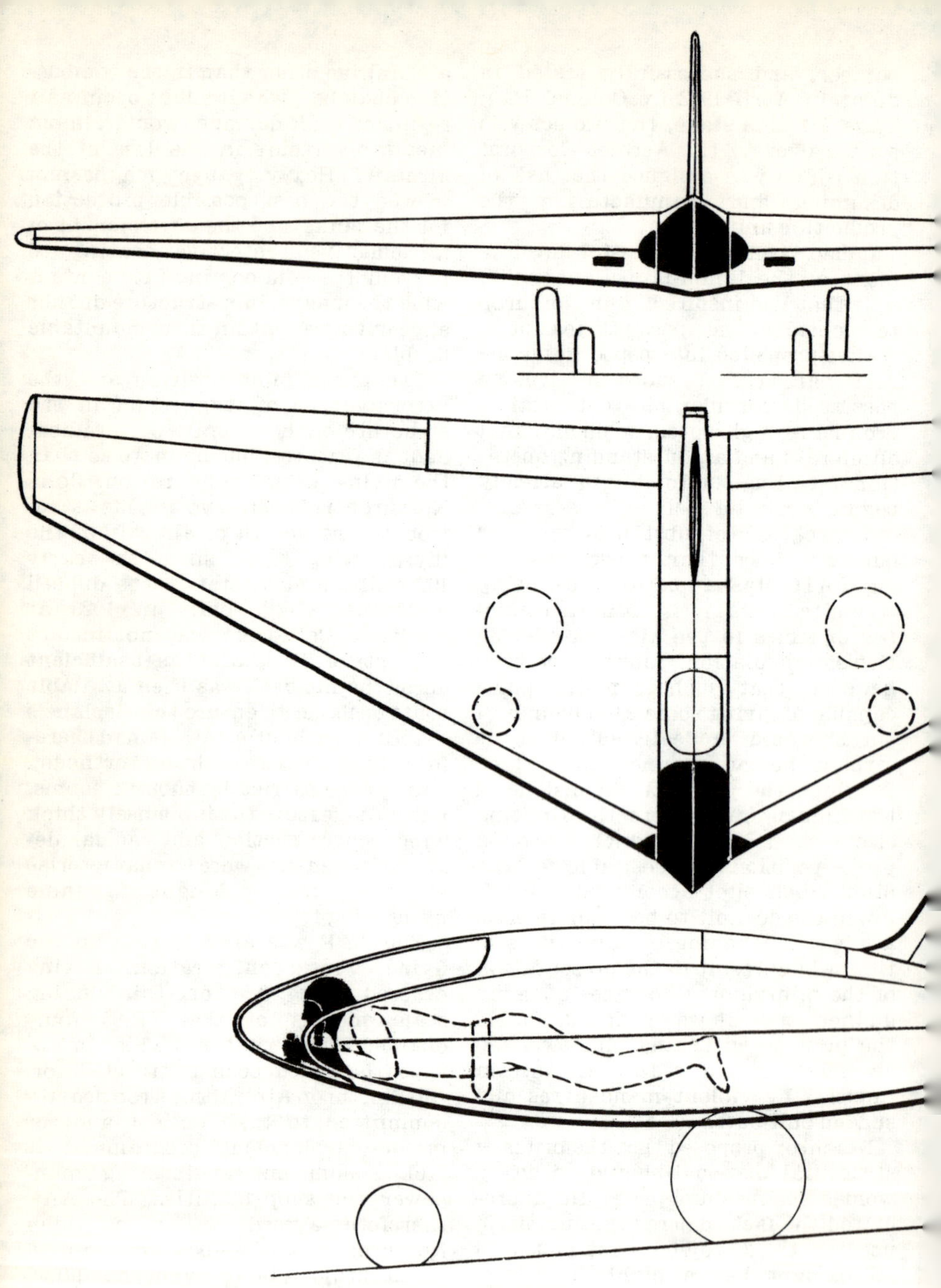

One of the most exotic interceptor fighters ever designed, the Northrop XP-79 rocket-driven interceptor was scrapped owing to the inability of Aerojet to perfect its power plant. These drawings (the side view is not to scale) reveal the XP-79's remarkably clean lines

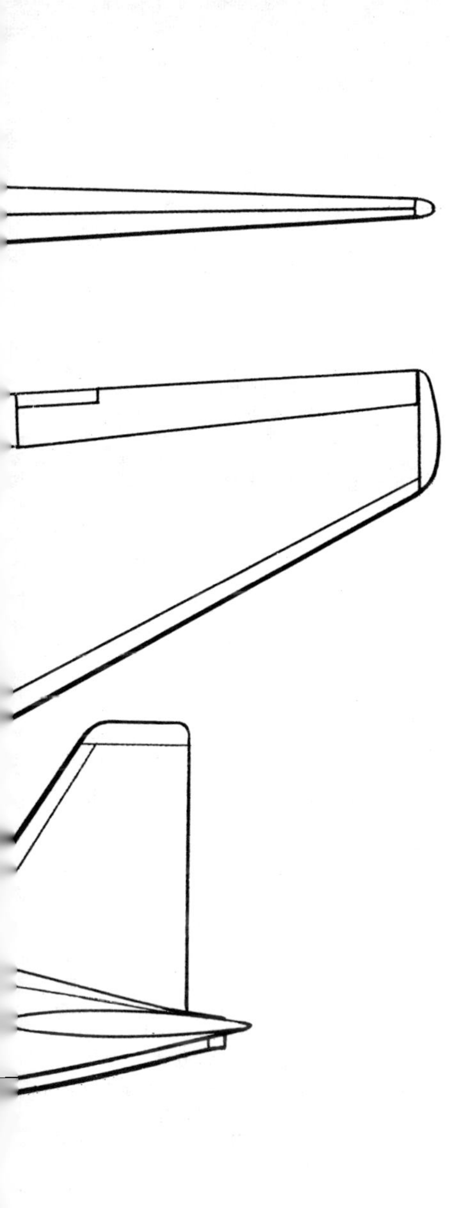

three prototype airplanes under the designation XP-79, a static test airframe, wind tunnel models, and engineering data was initiated. At that stage in the war, Northrop Aircraft was severely restricted in its choice of sub-contractors but selected Avion Incorporated which was occupying the Gaffers and Sattler Stove Factory in Los Angeles, and which included on its staff a number of engineers formerly with Vultee Aircraft. At the same time, the decision was taken to build three full-scale wooden flying mock-ups of the interceptor.

The detailed model specification for the XP-79, submitted to the AAF Air Material Command on 1st April 1943, envisaged an airplane with a loaded weight of 11,400 pounds, its wing spanning thirty-six feet with root and tip chords of 136 inches and thirty-six inches respectively, an aspect ratio of 5.07 and a gross area of 255 square feet. Welded magnesium alloy was to be used throughout the basic wing structure which was a monocoque with skinning varying in thickness from three-quarters of an inch at the leading edge to three-sixteenths at the trailing edge. The centre section, eight feet in width, was to house the pilot's cockpit, the rocket motor, the aniline tanks and the armament, and the major portion of the outer panels was to be occupied by the oxidant tanks.

All movable control surfaces were also to be of welded magnesium alloy, and these were to consist of elevons for pitch and roll extending over some sixty per cent of the wing, and split-type manoeuvre brakes extending outboard from the centre line of the airplane over approximately forty per cent of the semi-span. The pilot was to be provided with a crossbar with hand grips for operating the elevons, pitch being obtained by movement of the crossbar fore and aft, and roll by movement of the crossbar on its horizontal axis. The manoeuvre brakes were to be controlled manually by foot pedals

One of the MX-324 gliders fitted with the unsuccessful take-off trolley

but with sufficient power boost to reduce the operating loads to a reasonable level, this boost being obtained from dynamic air pressure acting on an internal bellows within the manoeuvre brakes themselves.

The pilot's cockpit was to be sealed to form a pressurised capsule capable of withstanding 2.75 pounds per square inch, but no means of actually pressurising the cockpit were to be provided. Armament was to comprise four 0.5-inch calibre M2 machine guns on E10 recoil - absorbing adapters, two on either side of the longitudinal axis of the airplane just outboard of the aniline tanks, and provision was to be made for carrying 250 rounds of ammunition per gun.

Apart from the thick magnesium alloy skins, armour was to be provided in the form of a quarter-inch face-hardened steel plate, inserted just inside the wing leading edge, at forty-five degrees to the chord plane, and extending from the side of the aniline tank adjacent to the cockpit to the outboard side of the main nitric acid tanks, plus a bullet-resistant glass screen to protect the pilot from forward fire.

The Aerojet rocket motor, which had been dubbed a 'Rotojet', was to be located on the centre line of the airplane immediately aft of the cockpit, and this used propellant pumps driven through a gear train which was connected to a thrust chamber assembly that rotated during engine operation. This assembly comprised four thrust units, two developing 750 pounds of thrust each and the remaining two each developing 250 pounds, resulting in a total thrust of 2,000 pounds. Each of the chamber nozzles was canted to provide a rotating force, all being coupled together to rotate as a complete assembly. The propellants were fed to the chambers by the pumps through a rotating shaft comprising two

concentric tubes with the appropriate propellant seals. For take-off, the thrust of the 'Rotojet' was to be augmented by six 1,000-pound thrust, solid-propellant JATO units which were to be jettisoned as soon as their fuel had been exhausted.

Provision was to be made for an 8,400-pound load of oxidant and fuel in a ratio of 1.75 to one, the aniline tanks having a total capacity of 262.6 US gallons and the oxidant tanks having a total capacity of 468 US gallons – the latter being separated from the former by the gun bays.

In March 1943 it was decided to modify the third XP-79 to incorporate two Westinghouse 19-B axial-flow turbojets in place of the Aerojet rocket motor. The modified airplane was designated XP-79B, but primary emphasis remained on the rocket-driven XP-79, and on 3rd June 1943 a 'Limited Engineering Inspection' of the XP-79 was held, this taking the place of the normal 'Mock-up Inspection' owing to the strict secrecy attached to the project. It was concluded during the inspection that the XP-79 bid fair to provide an outstanding performance, although certain deficiencies – resulting from the use of a rocket motor and a prone position for the pilot – would have to be resolved before the interceptor could be accepted for AAF service. The major problem was the method of supporting the pilot's head to withstand the accelerations in excess of twelve-g that the XP-79 was expected to achieve, and the AeroMedical Laboratory at Wright Field was asked to undertake research into permissible prone pilot accelerations and to assist the contractor in developing an adequate method of support. The University of Southern California was also contacted with reference to this problem, and, with the contractor, eventually evolved a method enabling the pilot to take twelve-g positive acceleration yet still operate the flying controls normally.

By July it became apparent that Aerojet was having difficulty in finalising the design of the 'Rotojet' rocket motor, and Avion advised the Air Material Command that delivery of the first XP-79 would be postponed from the contractual delivery date of 30th September until 15th December 1943. Subsequently, in September, the estimated delivery date was again revised – this time to 15th January 1944. Meanwhile, a revised specification for the XP-79 had been submitted on 5th August. The design gross weight had escalated to 11,893 pounds, the overall dimensions had been slightly increased, span and gross wing area had been raised to thirty-eight feet and 278 square feet respectively, and the root chord had been increased to 141.7 inches, although the tip chord had been reduced to thirty-four inches. The estimated performance for the XP-79 now included a maximum speed of 518mph at 40,000 feet, and a cruising speed at that altitude (at a weight of 5,500

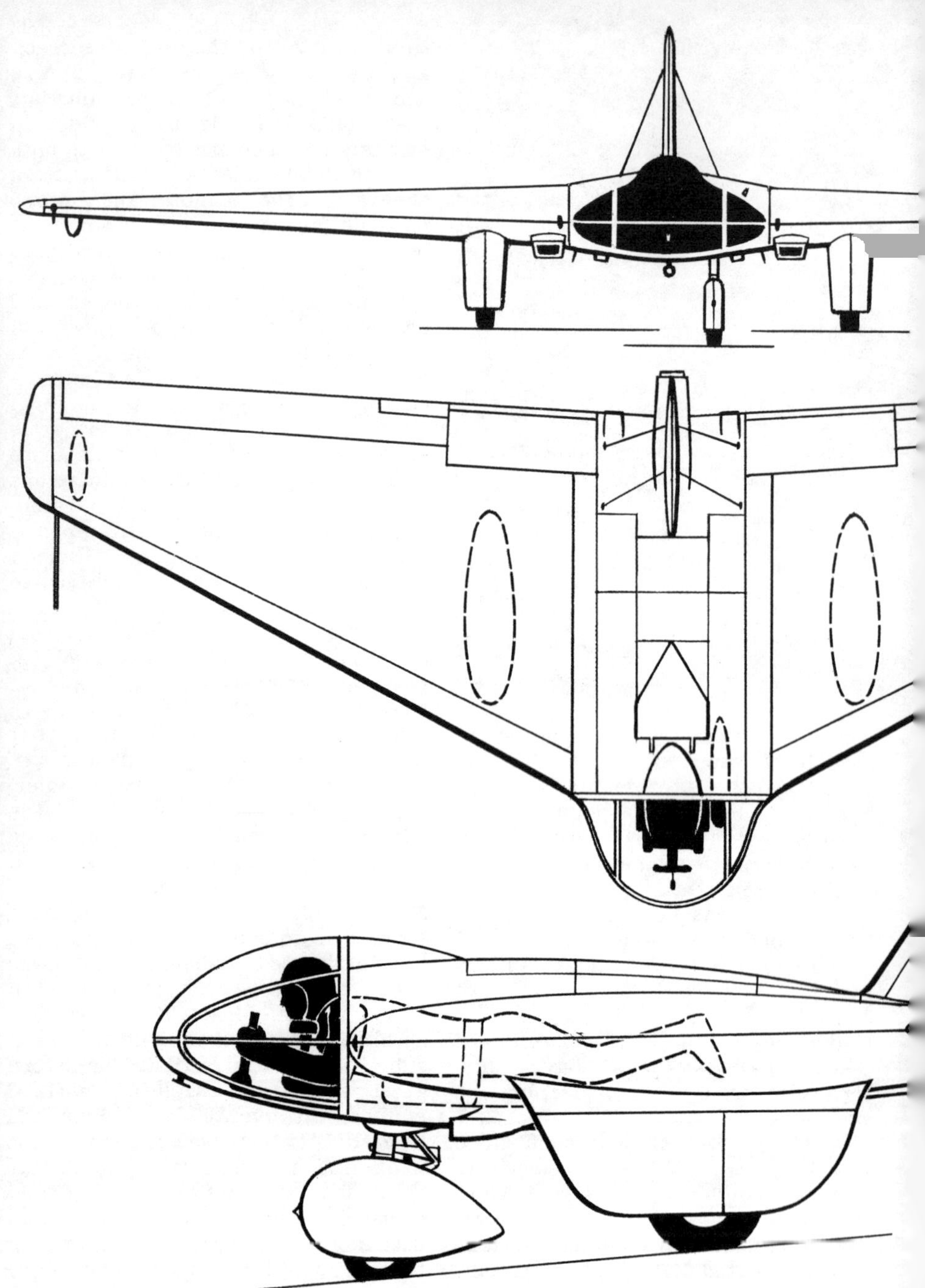

The Northrop MX-324, the first aircraft to be flown solely under rocket power in the USA. It was a near-full-scale model of the XP-79 interceptor. These drawings show the position adopted by pilot (note that the sideview is not to scale), and the fixed tricycle undercarriage

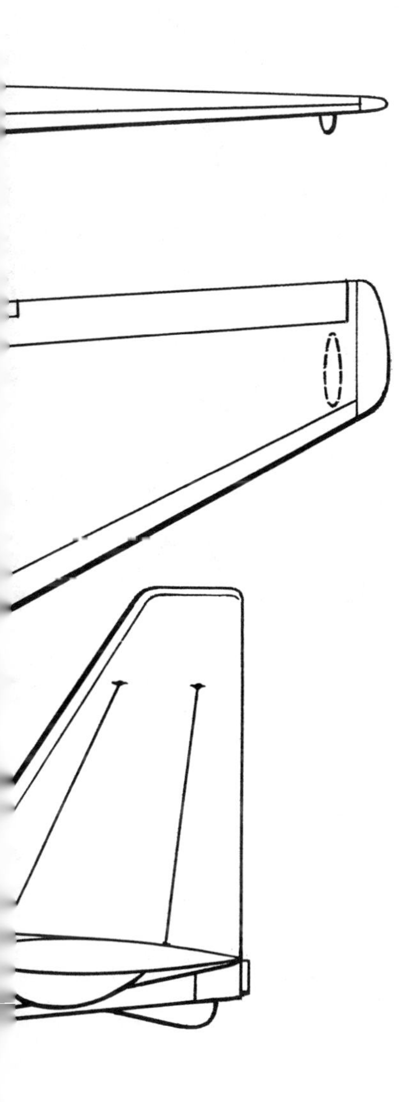

pounds and using 300 pounds of thrust) of 433mph. After take-off and acceleration to best climbing speed at sea level, it was calculated that the XP-79 would attain an altitude of 40,000 feet in seven minutes, and that endurance at this altitude at minimum cruising thrust would be 31.4 minutes. In the light of later knowledge, it was to be seen that these estimated figures were somewhat optimistic.

Delay followed delay. Avion submitted numerous generalised reports on the XP-79 and various aspects of its development to the Air Material Command, who considered them to be of no more than academic interest insofar as the project was concerned, and who were finally prompted to instruct Avion to terminate 'all unnecessary work' in order to concentrate its effort on building a flyable airplane.

In November 1943, the armament section mockup was shipped to Wright Field where, after test firing, it was pronounced satisfactory, but in December the estimated first flight date of the XP-79 was again revised, this time owing to delays in the delivery of the rocket motor. A date of 15th April 1944 was now promised, based on delivery of the Aerojet power plant one month earlier.

While the XP-79 had been pursuing its chequered career through drawing board and fabrication phases, tests had begun with the wooden flying scale models which had been assigned the cryptic designation MX-324 and, to confuse matters even further, were referred to as 'Project 12' for security reasons. The first of the trio of MX-324 gliders was fitted with skids and was intended to be towed at high speed behind a car, but owing to the weight of the glider the car was unable to attain a sufficient speed for the MX-324 to become airborne. The second MX-324 was fitted with a four-wheel detachable trolley but this proved to be unsatisfactory, and the third had a fixed tricycle undercarriage which spoiled the lines of the aircraft but at least enabled it to be towed from the ground. The first gliding flight was made on 2nd October 1943 with John Myers at the controls.

From the outset, it had been planned to apply rocket power to the MX-324, and Aerojet had been developing a small acid-aniline motor, the XCAL-200 of 200 pounds thrust, specifically for installation in the glider, this power plant being known at Aerojet Engineering's Azusa plant simply as 'Project X'. The XCAL-200 had a cast aluminium combustion chamber and was restartable in the air but weighed as much as 427 pounds. Like the larger, more sophisticated motor that Aerojet was struggling to produce for the XP-79, the XCAL-200 had its quota of problems, and its delivery was progressively delayed. Meanwhile, gliding trials with the MX-324 continued.

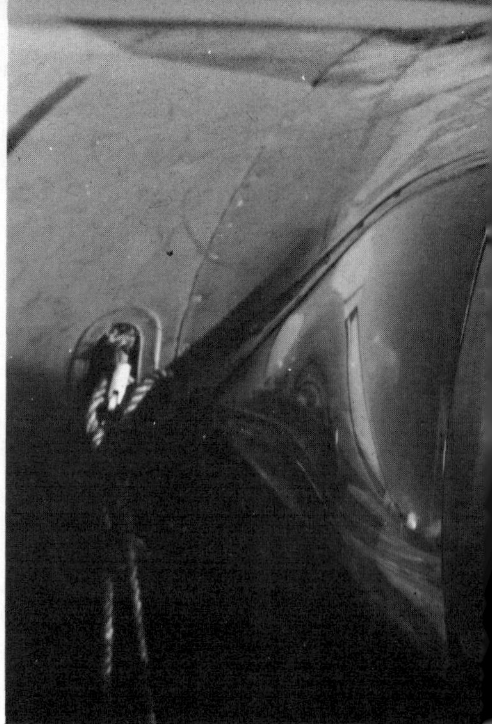

At this time it was believed that controllability of the XP-79 would benefit from fixed slats at the extremities of the wing, and for one flight test the MX-324 was fitted with such slats to evaluate their efficacy. This flight nearly ended in tragedy, although the accident was in no way due to the slats which, in any case, were subsequently to be discarded as unnecessary. On this occasion the MX-324 had been towed to an altitude of some 10,000 feet, and after casting off the towline, the pilot inadvertently released the escape hatches while banking steeply, partially falling from the airplane.

His instinctive grasp on the crossbar control produced an incredible wing-over, and when things calmed down the pilot found himself hanging upside down from his harness, his head and trunk suspended beneath the aircraft which had entered a steady inverted glide. The minor movements of the crossbar of which he was capable seemed to produce little effect, and very much shaken, he eventually succeeded in pulling himself onto the leading edge of the centre section where he sat while he checked his chute harness. He then slid off the wing and made a normal parachute descent. The MX-324, apparently undisturbed by the change in the centre of gravity resulting from its pilot's departure, continued its inverted glide in a wide circle, finally landing upside-down a short distance from the point from which it had originally taken off. It suffered some damage but this proved easily repairable, and the pilot was no worse off for his unnerving experience – if somewhat embarrassed by the incident.

The XCAL-200 motor had attained sufficient reliability to permit its installation in the MX-324 by the spring of 1944, and was housed neatly in the wing centre section immediately aft of the pilot's cockpit, with an aniline tank and two nitric acid tanks on either side. The only outward signs of this metamorphosis from glider to rocket-driven airplane was the rocket exhaust pipe beneath the vertical stabiliser, and the adjacent steam vent pipe. Although the MX-324 had originally been

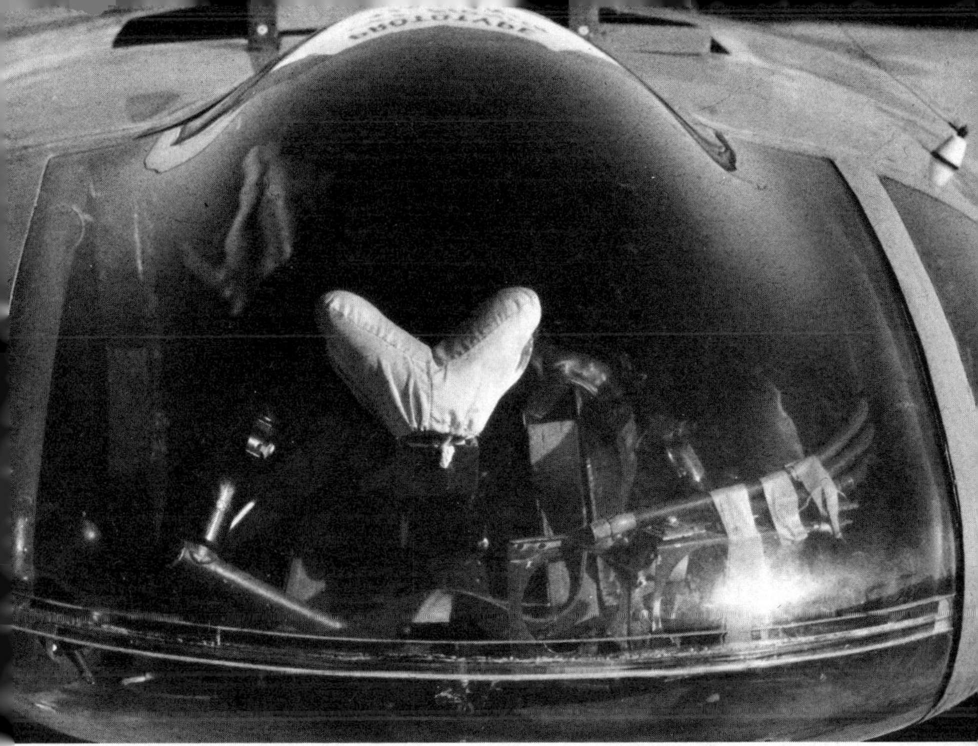

This view of the nose of the MX-324 clearly shows the pilot's chin rest

intended as a full-scale flying mock-up of the XP-79, it was, in fact, somewhat smaller, spanning thirty-two feet and having an overall length of twelve feet. Complete with rocket motor and full aniline and nitric acid tanks it weighed 3,656 pounds.

Once the installation of the rocket motor, the acid-aniline tanks, and the necessary feedlines and controls had been completed, the MX-324 was taken to Harper's Dry Lake, a remote portion of the California desert, near Barstow. Ground runs of the rocket motor began on 20th June 1944. Two days later, the rocket was run at full power with the airplane tethered to the ground, and on 23rd June, Northrop's test pilot, Harry Crosby, made the first taxying trials.

A few modifications were made as a result of these, and on the morning of 5th July, the MX-324, with Crosby lying on his stomach, his chin supported by a padded rest which enabled him to look straight ahead without undue strain, was towed off the ground to an altitude of 8,000 feet at which point the towline was cast off. Crosby pressed the starter trigger of the rocket motor, and belching a stream of fire and black smoke, the little airplane accelerated to nearly 270mph before its fuel was exhausted and the rocket cut out, Crosby gliding gently down to make a perfect landing. The XCAL-200 rocket motor had run for 4.3 minutes, and the first manned rocket-driven aircraft in the USA had flown successfully. But in view of the secrecy attached to the project, this fact was known to few other people than the handful of AAF, Avion, Northrop and Aerojet Engineering personnel who had witnessed the event.

Harry Crosby made several other successful flights in the rocket-driven MX-324 which was usually towed off the ground by a P-38 Lightning, but it was obvious that the

The rocket-propelled MX-324 test airplane flown under power in July 1944

XCAL-200 was insufficiently powerful to enable higher speeds to be attained, and Aerojet Engineering had been unable to develop a more powerful motor offering acceptable standards of reliability. A few weeks after Harry Crosby's pioneering flight the entire XP-79 programme was abandoned.

Work on the 'Rotojet' rocket motor for the XP-79 at Aerojet's California plant had fallen further and further behind. As one problem was solved, another appeared to take its place, and in view of these delays, in March the Air Material Command had decided to switch priority from the rocket-driven XP-79 to the turbojet-powered XP-79B. Avion had been scheduled to receive a mock-up Westinghouse 19-B turbojet on about 15th April, Northrop estimating that the XP-79B would be ready to make its first flight on 1st August 1944.

The continuation of work on the rocket-driven XP-79 had still appeared desirable, particularly in view of intelligence reports concerning German developments in the field of rocket-propelled interceptors, but in June the Air Material Command had begun to receive disquieting reports from the Western District Engineering Officer of the situation developing in the Los Angeles plant of Avion Incorporated. These referred to singularly high wastage, undesirable shop practices, and extremely low morale, placing the entire XP-79 programme in jeopardy.

A Northrop engineer was hurriedly put in charge at Avion, but yet another obstacle was now placed in front of the AAF's first rocket-driven interceptor: Aerojet Engineering informed the Command that the company was unable to solve certain of the most fundamental problems posed by the development of the 'Rotojet' motor. The Command now had no option but to tacitly admit

defeat, and accordingly, in September 1944 barely a month after the Luftwaffe had committed rocket-propelled interceptors to combat – both XP-79 prototypes and the static test airplane were cancelled. Thus, US efforts to develop a rocket-driven fighter had ended in abysmal failure through no fault of concept or aerodynamic design – indeed, the XP-79 was aesthetically one of the most beautiful and aerodynamically one of the most efficient warplanes designed during the Second World War – but through the shortcomings of existing US rocket motor technology.

The fall-out from this programme, the turbojet-powered XP-79B, was to fare little better than the rocket-driven interceptor from which it stemmed. Transferred from Avion to Northrop's plant at Hawthorne, California, on 1st December 1944, it was eventually to be completed and shipped to Muroc Dry Lake from where it was to be flown on 12th September 1945 by Harry Crosby, the pilot who had performed the rocket-propelled flights in the MX-324 fourteen months earlier. The airplane flew successfully for fourteen minutes. Crosby had executed a number of manoeuvres when, at an altitude of some 7,000 feet, the XP-79B appeared to execute a slow roll from which it failed to recover, hitting the ground in a spin. Crosby was seen to leave the airplane at about 2,000 feet but appeared to be struck by the gyrating prototype before he could open his parachute, and fell to his death. A subsequent inquiry into the accident failed to reach a definite conclusion as to its cause, although it was believed that an electrically controlled trim tab had failed to work and that the pilot had been unable to overcome the asymmetric forces in which this malfunction had resulted. This accident was to be one of the first nails to be knocked into the coffin of John Northrop's aspirations for aircraft of flying wing concept.

The fall-out from the XP-79 programme, the turbojet-powered XP-79B fighter

352437
211742

The Komet committed

At the end of February 1944, while the Air Material Command was reluctantly concluding that it would be advisable, in view of Aerojet's difficulties, to switch priorities from the rocket-driven XP-79 to the turbojet-propelled XP-79B, the first 'sharp starts' were being performed with production Komet interceptors by three civilian test pilots, Karl Voy, Franz Perschall, and Herbert Lamm, who had first undergone a three-week familiarisation course with EK 16 at Bad Zwischenahn. The initiation of production testing was seriously behind schedule; the first of the series interceptors – designated Me 163B-1a to distinguish them from the Messerschmitt-built pre-series Me 163Ba-1 – had presented the test personnel with innumerable headaches. These airplanes had been assembled in the Black Forest from components manufactured by a number of factories, several of which were inexperienced in working to close tolerances. From the Black Forest they had been transported in sealed and closely-guarded wagons to Lechfeld from where they were supposed to be test flown. However, a host of minor modifications had been found necessary upon arrival, and the flight test programme had been delayed for some months while these modifications were made.

The production Me 163B-1a differed from the pre-production Me 163Ba-1, only in that it substituted 30mm MK 108 cannon for the 20mm MG 151 weapons previously installed and that it was fitted with an HWK 509A-1 or -2 rocket motor (the production version of the R II-211) providing 3,750 pounds of thrust. Sixty rounds of ammunition were provided for each of the MK 108s, the shells being carried in two boxes located under a detachable fairing aft of the aerial mast for the FuG 16zy radio. A compressed air bottle to cock the cannon was mounted below and aft of each weapon, and the guns were aimed by means of a Revi 16B reflector sight attached to a removable mounting on the base of the 90mm armourglass windscreen. Protection for the pilot was afforded by a 15mm armour nose cone, 13mm head and shoulder armour segments, and an 8mm armour backplate. In addition to the FuG 16zy ultra-short-wave radio for plane-to-plane and plane-to-ground communication, which incorporated direction and range measuring facilities, the Me 163B-1a was fitted with FuG 25a as recognition equipment for anti-aircraft batteries and as a direction indicator for the ground station.

The cockpit was enclosed by a mechanically-jettisonable hinged Plexiglas moulded canopy through which the pilot enjoyed an excellent field of vision. The instrument panel carried rate-of-climb, turn-and-bank, and altitude-compensated airspeed indicators, a fine-course altimeter and a temperature gauge. There were two pressure gauges on the starboard side of the main panel, and a small panel on the port side of the cockpit carried the control quadrant for operating the retractable landing skid which was activated by an accumulator-pressurised hydraulic system. A pull-out handle for emergency fuel jettisoning and a cock for the emergency jettisoning of the twin-wheel take-off dolly by air pressure were mounted beside the quadrant.

The pilot's seat was torsion-sprung and capable of absorbing an impact of more than twenty-g, having been designed along the lines suggested by Dr Justus Schneider after his investigation of the injuries suffered by Dittmar and Opitz. In other respects it was conventional, and adjustable for height only. On either side of the seat was a sixteen US gallon self-sealing T-Stoff tank, and immediately aft was the main unprotected 275 US gallon T-Stoff tank. All C-Stoff was accommodated in the wings, this comprising two nineteen US gallon leading-edge tanks and two forty-six gallon tanks aft of the mainspar, none of which was protected. The three T-Stoff tanks were interconnected and filled through a single cap located behind the aerial mast, and the two C-Stoff tanks in each wing were connected by a balance pipe and fed into a small collector tank in the fuselage under pressure. Drain plugs were located in the base of the skid fairing to allow the fuel tanks to be flushed out after each flight.

The HWK 509A rocket motor weighed only 220 pounds complete, and consisted of two principal assemblies, the forward assembly comprising the turbine housing, the worm-type fuel pumps geared to the turbine shaft, the control box, a pressure-reducing valve, and the electric starter motor, and the aft assembly being formed by the combustion chamber unit which was connected to the forward assembly by means of a cylindrical tube through which pipes carried fuel to the individual jets. The fuselage was an oval-section, stressed-skin, light alloy structure, and the wings were of wooden construction with a single mainspar at approximately quarter-chord, and an auxiliary rear spar carying the fabric-covered elevons and the large trimming surfaces inboard. These balanced out the split flaps located well forward to minimise pitching movement when deflected for landing. The wings, which had plywood skinning, were swept 23.3 degrees at quarter-chord, this being sufficient to allow a fore and aft displacement of the elevons in order that they could act as elevators but insufficient to boost the critical Mach number.

The two-wheel undercarriage dolly was connected to the rear portion of the landing skid housing by two lugs which engaged mechanical catches, these being automatically disconnected to jettison the dolly on retraction of the skid. For landing the main skid was supplemented by small wingtip skids which protected the wingtips when one or other of these scraped along the ground once speed had fallen below the minimum at which the pilot could keep the airplane level. A light three-wheeled tractor known as a Scheuschlepper was used for towing the Komet on the ground, a rigid towbar connecting with a towing point in the skid fairing. A special trailer could be towed by the Scheuschlepper for retrieving the Komet once it had landed, this trailer being equipped with hydraulic arms which raised the aircraft so that its skid rested between the trailer's two caterpillar tracks.

The pilot's equipment included a protective overall manufactured of Asbestos-Mipolamfibre which was theoretically acid proof, and was intended to provide some protection

A Komet is towed to take-off point by a 'Scheuschlepper' (above), and returns to the maintenance hangars after retrieval by special trailer (below)

in the event of T-Stoff finding its way into the cockpit. Protective clothing of similar material was also worn by ground personnel during refuelling operations. One of the civilian test pilots, Karl Voy, described the flight testing of the production Komets as follows: 'For reasons of safety and to save fuel, each aircraft was flown in unpowered form before a 'sharp start' was risked, the Komet being towed from the ground by a Bf 110. After take-off, a Scheuschlepper drove to the other end of the runway to retrieve the take-off dolly, and following the landing, the same Scheuschlepper jacked up the airplane so that the dolly could be refitted, and then towed the Komet back to the apron. Some Komets could be accepted as ready for a 'sharp start' after only one gliding test, but others – the so-called 'cripples' – demanded seven or eight towed starts before they could be considered safe for powered flight, and it was our task to pass only safe airplanes to the Luftwaffe.'

'These gliding trials called for no special preparations, but "sharp starts" were another matter entirely, demanding elaborate safety precautions. Because of the considerable fire hazard, a fast foam-extinguisher tender was always ready on the starting line with engine running, this being accompanied by an ambulance complete with doctor and medical staff. In the event of an accident, it was vital that skilled medical aid be on the spot owing to the highly corrosive and inflammable properties of the rocket fuels. There was also a "turnover" vehicle parked at the other side of the field – a pick-up truck fitted with a hoist. The "turnover" truck was used to lift an overturned airplane after a mishap during take-off or landing in order to release the trapped pilot. This task had to be performed with the utmost speed, as even after completing a powered flight, some fuel remained in the tanks, sometimes more than fifty US gallons, and this could well explode or ooze over the trapped pilot with horrifying results.'

'Owing to the ever-present possibility of leaks in the fuel system and the fire danger in consequence, the Komet was tanked-up only on the day that it was to fly; no tanked-up aircraft were allowed to stand in a hangar. Before a "sharp start" the Komet was anchored to the ground and the rocket motor ignited for a brief test run. The tanks were then topped up, and the pilot, in his Asbestos-Mipolamfibre overall, climbed into the cockpit, fastened his harness, and checked his oxygen and R/T equipment. The oxygen mask was worn all the time because of the possibility of fumes seeping into the cockpit. The control lever was then set to idling position, opening the fuel cocks and engaging the electric starter motor. The motor rotated the turbine shafts and pumps, thus priming the system, and once a sufficient head of steam had been generated to drive the turbine at a speed at which the T-Stoff was forced through the pressure reducing-valve (approximately forty per cent revs), the rocket motor began to operate normally. When revs attained seventy per cent, the thrust control lever could be moved forward one-third of its travel, at which point the rocket ignited. The thrust control was then slowly moved to its maximum forward position, and when the specified pressure was reached in the combustion chamber, you were ready to go.'

'For take-off the Komet was trimmed tail heavy, and it was standard practice to jettison the twin-wheel dolly as soon as an altitude of twenty to thirty feet had been reached, the landing skid and tailwheel retracting simultaneously. If the jettisoning gear malfunctioned we were instructed to abandon the airplane as the chances of making a successful landing with the dolly in position were negligible, as Hanna Reitsch had

Messerschmit Me 163B-1a

1 Generator drive propeller
2 Generator
3 Cockpit ventilation intake
4 Compressed air bottle
5 Battery and electronic packs
6 15mm solid armour nose-cone
7 Accumulator-pressuriser
8 Direct cockpit air intake
9 FuG 25A radio pack
10 Plastic rudder pedals
11 Rudder control assembly
12 Hydraulic and compressed air points
13 Control relay
14 T-Stoff cockpit tank (port)
15 Flying controls assembly box
16 Radio tuning controls
17 Control column
18 Hinged instrument panel
19 Revi 16B gunsight
20 90mm armour glass screen
21 Armament and radio switches
22 Pilot's seat
23 8mm back armour
24 13mm head and shoulder armour
25 Head rest
26 Mechanically jettisonable canopy
27 Ventilation panel
28 Fixed leading-edge wing slot
29 Trim tab
30 Fabric-covered elevon
31 Inboard trim flap
32 Position of underwing landing flap
33 Radio frequency selector pack
34 FuG 16ZY radio receiving aerial
35 T-Stoff filler cap
36 Fuselage T-Stoff tank

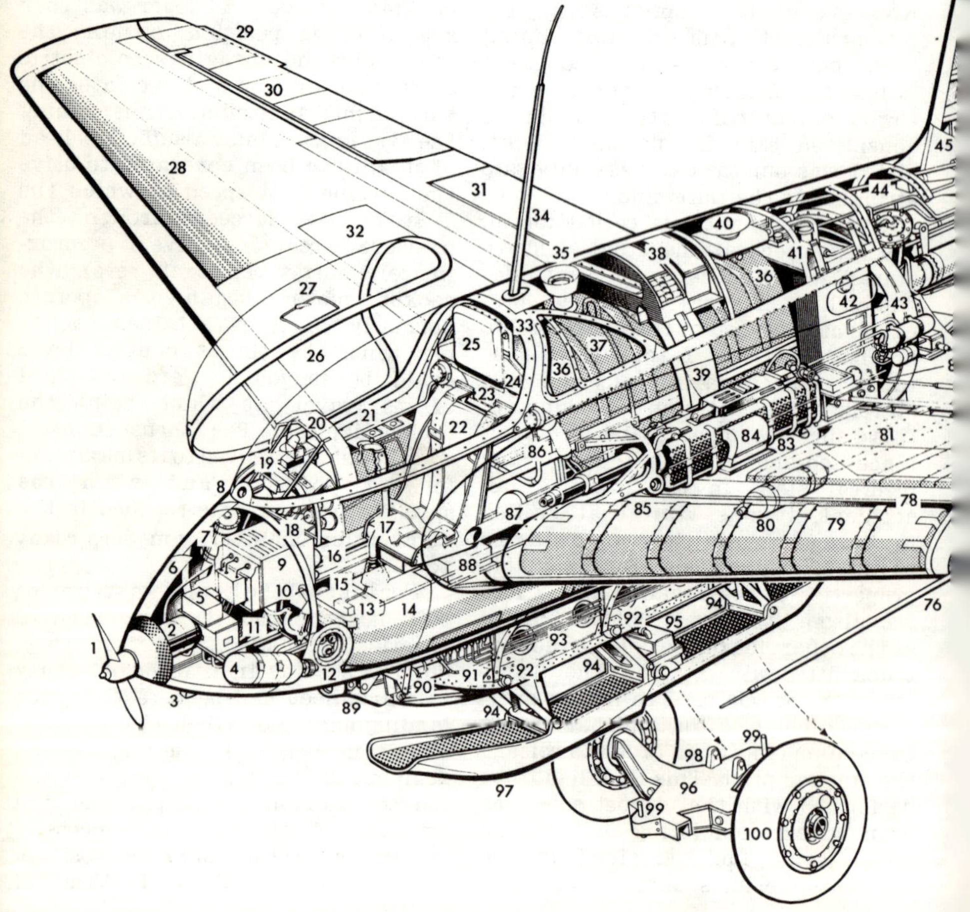

37 Aft cockpit glazing
38 Ammunition for MK 108 cannon
39 Ammunition feed chute
40 T-Stoff starter tank
41 C-Stoff filler cap
42 HWK 509A-1 motor turbine housing
43 Main rocket-motor mounting frame
44 Rudder control rod
45 Aerial matching unit
46 Tailfin construction
47 Rudder horn balance
48 Upper hinge to rudder
49 Rudder
50 Rudder trim tab
51 Rudder control rocker-bar
52 Rocket-motor combustion chamber
53 Tailpipe
54 Rocket thrust orifice
55 Vent pipe outlet
56 Hydraulic cylinder
57 Lifting point
58 Tailwheel fairing
59 Steerable tailwheel
60 Tailwheel oleo
61 Tailwheel steering linkage
62 Combustion chamber bracing
63 Wing fillet
64 Trim flap mounting
65 Inboard trim flap
66 Elevon mounting
67 Port elevon
68 Trim tab
69 Rear wing spar
70 Wing tip bumper
71 Wing construction
72 Fixed leading-edge wing slot
73 Elevon actuator linkage
74 Position of port underwing flap
75 FuG 25A aerial
76 Pitot head
77 Wing tank connecting pipe
78 Front wing spar

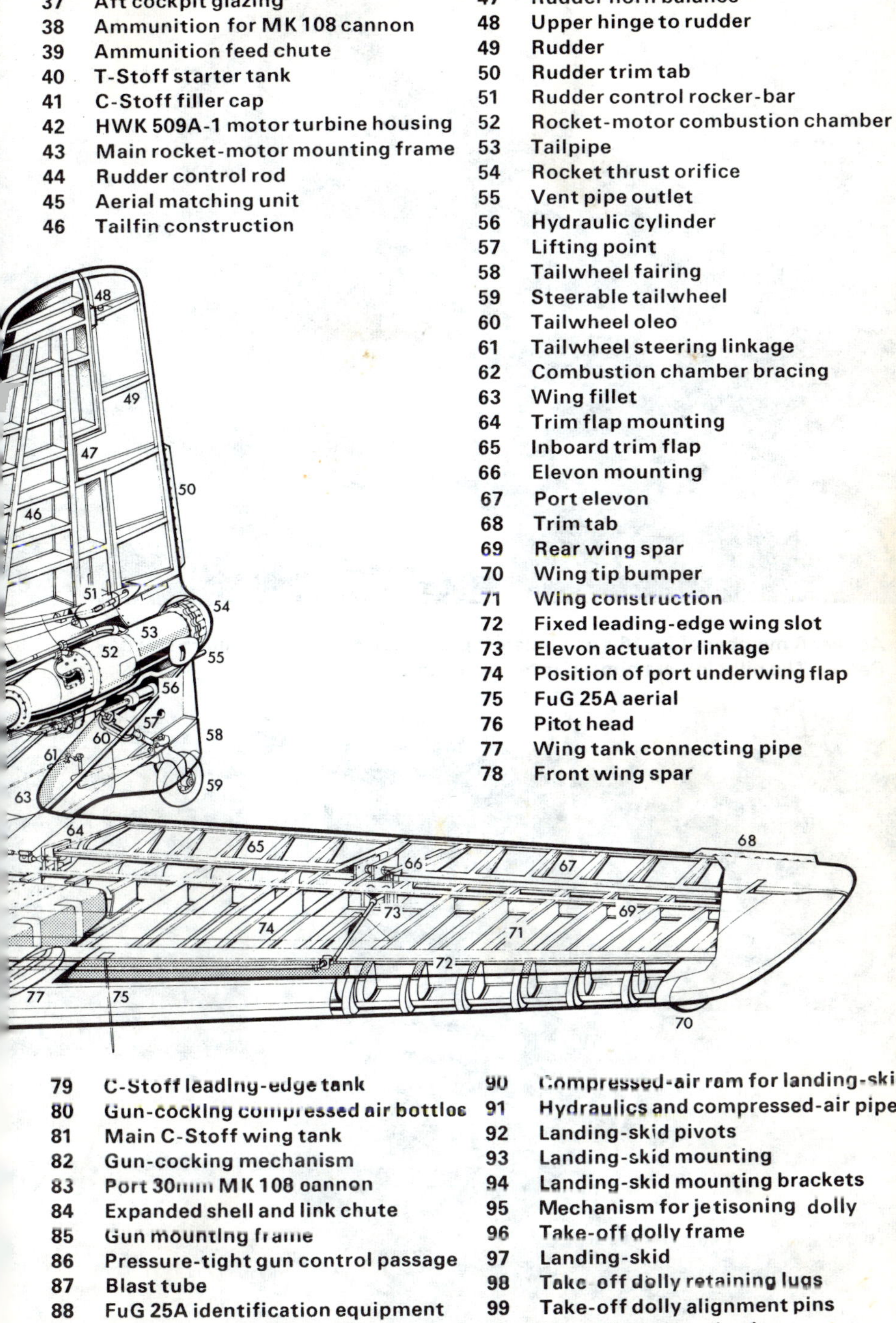

79 C-Stoff leading-edge tank
80 Gun-cocking compressed air bottles
81 Main C-Stoff wing tank
82 Gun-cocking mechanism
83 Port 30mm MK 108 cannon
84 Expanded shell and link chute
85 Gun mounting frame
86 Pressure-tight gun control passage
87 Blast tube
88 FuG 25A identification equipment
89 Tow-bar attachment point
90 Compressed-air ram for landing-skid
91 Hydraulics and compressed-air pipes
92 Landing-skid pivots
93 Landing-skid mounting
94 Landing-skid mounting brackets
95 Mechanism for jetisoning dolly
96 Take-off dolly frame
97 Landing-skid
98 Take-off dolly retaining lugs
99 Take-off dolly alignment pins
100 Large diameter wheels

Above: **A member of EK 16's groundstaff prepares a Komet for a 'sharp start'.**
Below: **The pilot lowers himself into the cockpit**

Above: A member of the groundstaff assists the pilot to adjust his oxygen mask prior to a 'sharp start'. *Below:* The Komet begins its take-off run

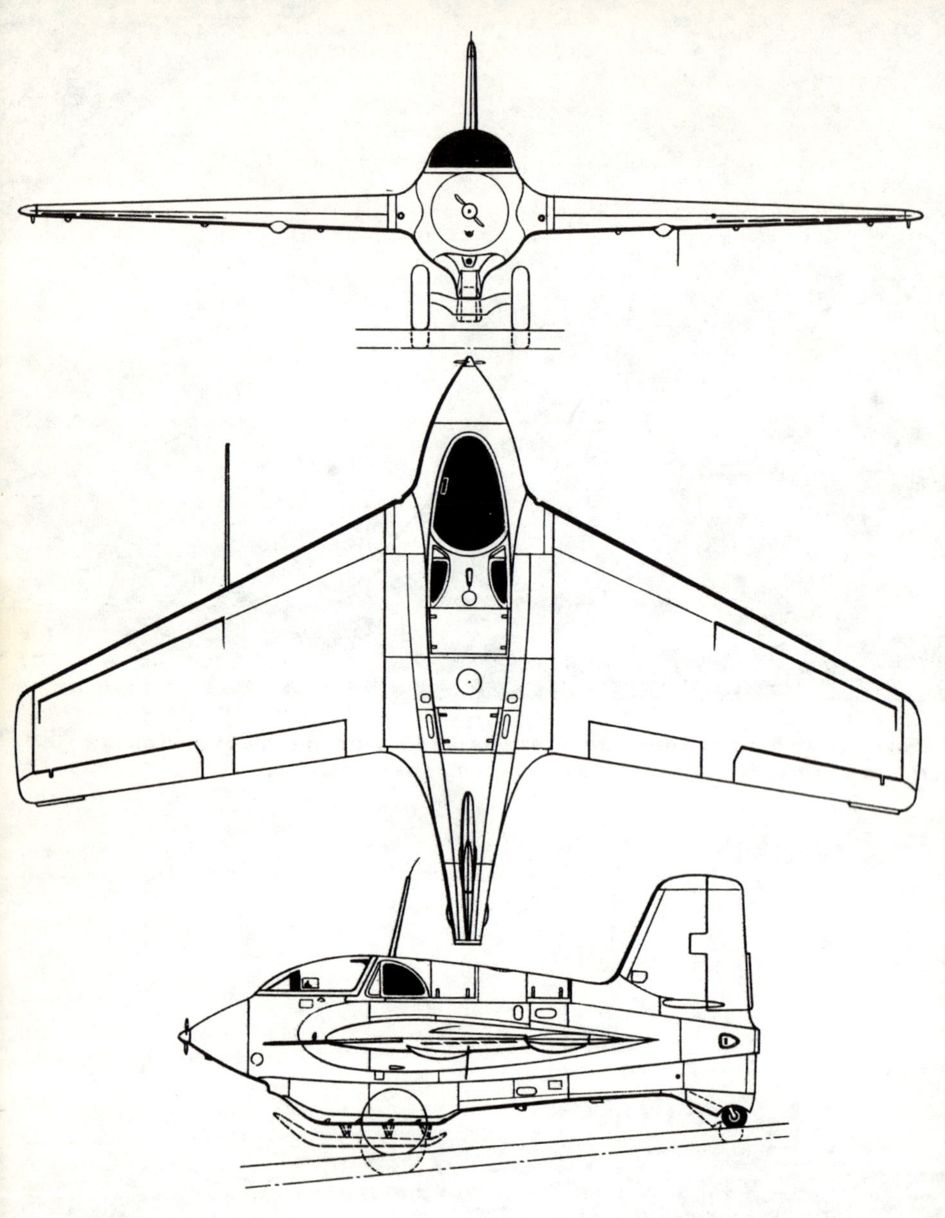

Me 163B-1a specification : ***Power Plant :*** **One 3,750 lb thrust Walter 509A rocket motor.** ***Weights :*** **Empty equipped, 4,200 lb, maximum loaded, 9,500 lb.** ***Performance :*** **Maximum speed, 515 mph at sea level, 596mph between 10,000 and 30,000 feet, initial climb rate, 16,000 ft per min, time to 30,000 feet, 2.6 min, to 39,500 feet, 3.5 min, maximum powered endurance, 7 min 30 sec.** ***Dimensions :*** **Span, 39 ft 7⅓ in, length, 19 ft 2⅓ in, height, 9 ft 0⅓ in, wing area, 199.132 sq ft**

proved some time earlier. For a normal test the climbout was performed at a flat angle until an altitude of some 650 feet was reached. The speed was then allowed to build up to 465mph, at which the Komet was pulled up into a steep climb, and at a climbing angle of forty-five to fifty degrees an altitude of 39,370 feet could be reached in two and a half minutes. The test programme called for a high-speed dash up to 590mph at 19,685 feet, and, if all instruments and systems functioned efficiently during climb and speed trials, the Komet was declared "safe and ready for operational use". Frequently, however, as many as three "sharp starts" had to be performed with an airplane before this declaration could be made.'

The first production Me 163B-la was actually accepted by the Luftwaffe in May 1944, by which time production testing had been transferred from Lechfeld to Jesau, near Königsberg in East Prussia. Three Komets were accepted in June and twelve in July when EK 16 at Bad Zwischenahn began to receive production series airplanes, the first ten to arrive being tested personally by Opitz, who had recovered from his spinal injuries and returned to the Test Detachment. However, in May, Wolfgang Späte had been promoted to Major and posted to the Eastern Front as Commander of the IV Gruppe of Jagdgeschwader 54. His place as CO of EK 16 was taken by Hauptmann 'Toni' Thaler. The loss of Späte was considered a serious blow by the personnel of EK 16; it came at a time when this outstanding combat pilot's experience would have been invaluable in the working-up of the Komet to operational status.

The first simulated operational sortie mounted by EK 16 assumed that an enemy bomber formation was approaching at an altitude of 20,000-25,000 feet. The intercepting Komet took off, climbing at an angle of forty-five degrees to an altitude of 30,000 feet, but immediately the pilot levelled off the rocket motor cut out, and two or three minutes elapsed before it could be re-started. Owing to the danger of explosion in the event of any deviation from the set ratio of C-Stoff to T-Stoff, an automatic cut-out device was immediately activated if the flow in one of the feed-lines was interrupted for any reason. It was eventually discovered that the change in position of the fuel when the aircraft levelled out after its climb had produced an air lock which had activated the cut-out, and time-consuming modifications were necessary.

Plans for deployment of the Komet involved the preparation of two rings of bases in the west, north-west and north of Germany. The limited radius of action of the rocket-driven interceptors operating from these bases promised to overlap adequately for coverage of the complete area. In the event, the only airfields to receive the special storage facilities and other essentials which the operation demanded were to be Peenemünde, Bad Zwischenahn, Wittmundhafen, Udetfeld, Stargard, Deelen, Husum, and Venlo.

The first operational Komet squadron, 1 Staffel of the specially-created Jagdgeschwader 400, had in fact been formed at Wittmundhafen in May 1944, the nucleus of its personnel being drawn from EK 16. The Group Commander of Jagdgeschwader 400 was Major Robert Olejnik, who, prior to joining EK 16 in November 1943, had been Commander of the III Gruppe of Jagdgeschwader 1. He had been awarded the Knight's Cross of the Iron Cross in July 1941 at which time he had thirty-two confirmed 'kills' to his credit.

From the outset, the new Jagdgeschwader was to suffer misfortune. It did not receive its first Me 163B-la interceptors until July, and Olejnik himself elected to undertake the first 'sharp start' at Wittmundhafen. The Komet took-off successfully, jettisoned its twin-wheel dolly, gathered

speed and then began a forty-five degree climb. At an altitude of 10,000 feet the Komet appeared to falter, and from the irregular clouds of steam coming from the exhaust pipe it was obvious that the thrust of the rocket motor had begun to fluctuate strongly. Olejnik levelled off, simultaneously cutting the power plant, but then apparently attempted to re-ignite the rocket.

Almost immediately black smoke began to stream from the exhaust pipe, this quickly being joined by a whitish spray as Olejnik actuated the emergency fuel-dumping valve. The Komet turned in towards the field, streaming T-Stoff, and Olejnik jettisoned the cockpit canopy but made no attempt to abandon the stricken airplane. The Komet made a wide, slow circuit of the field but suddenly seemed to stagger.

The starboard wing dropped and Olejnik managed to right the plane just before it hit the ground. It rebounded into the air, hit the ground again, the port wing dug in and the

Above: **The Komet's cockpit**
Right: **The 'rocket-propelled flea' emblem of 2 Staffel of Jagdgeschwader 400**

Komet spun around. Olejnik, who had evidently released his harness, was thrown violently from the cockpit just as the airplane disappeared in a blinding explosion. Olejnik was fortunate in suffering no more than a broken vertebra, but his accident could hardly be taken by the new combat unit as a good omen.

Late in July, the 1 Staffel transferred from Wittmundhafen to Brandis, near Leipzig, and it was from this new base that the first combat sorties were flown, the first contact being made with the Americans on 28th July 1944 as previously recounted. Immediately after this first encounter with the Komet by the AAF, Major General William Kepner, commanding the fighter element of the Eighth Air Force, sent the following signal to all Groups: 'Five jet-propelled enemy aircraft, Me 163s, flying in two separate

formations, one element of two and one element of three, were seen in the target area around Merseburg.'

'The element of two was seen to approach the bombers from the rear at about 32,000 feet. They were leaving very dense white contrails. Their formation was reported as very good and they maintained formation position in their diving attack. They made a slight diving turn attack at the rear of the bombers at very high speed, reported as between 500 and 600mph. Eight of the 359th Group turned into them but they only turned slightly away and continued. The Group did not get a shot. After attacking, the jet wingman pulled up into the sun at a fifty-degree angle. In climb, the jet gave off smoke in bursts which was assumed to indicate the use of full power at intervals. It is believed that we can expect to see more of these aircraft immediately, and that we can expect attacks on the bombers from the rear in formations or waves.'

'To be able to counter and have time to turn into them, our units are going to have to be in positions relatively close to the bombers to be between them and our heavies. It is believed that these tactics will keep them from making effective, repeat effective, attacks on the bombers. Attention is called to the fact that probably the first thing seen will be dense contrails probably as high as 30,000 feet approaching from the rear of the bombers.'

Unbeknown to General Kepner, at the time his signal was sent, the Luftwaffe had accepted delivery of only sixteen production Komet interceptors. Even if the 1 Staffel of JG 400 had pressed home its attack, the chances of hitting one of the B-17s with the twin 30mm MK 108 cannon mounted by each of the rocket-propelled fighters were slender. At an approach speed of 560-590mph, the excess in speed over the target – a bomber formation flying at 220–250mph – was of the order of 340mph, and closing speed in an attack from the rear was virtually 500 feet per second.

Parked innocently around the perimeter of the airfield, Komet interceptors revealed no sign of their supreme volatility

As trials with the MK 108 cannon had already revealed, the minimum distance from which this weapon stood any chance of hitting a target of the size of a B-17 was 650 yards, and as evasive action had to be taken at 200 yards to avoid ramming the target, in an attack from the rear the pilot of the Komet had only the time that it took to traverse 450 yards – less than three seconds – to operate his slow-firing cannon. Only a combination of expert marksmanship and skilful flying afforded any likelihood of hitting the target. Furthermore, the MK 108 was not the most reliable of weapons, frequently jamming solid after the first few rounds had been fired.

Despite the shortcomings of its armament, the Komet enjoyed some success during its first weeks of operational service. As more aircraft were cleared for combat, AAF encounters with the 'powered egg' – as its pilots had now dubbed the Me 163B – became increasingly frequent; as JG 400 gained confidence in its mounts the tactics that it employed increased in variety. One mode of attack adopted by Komet pilots was to position their interceptors immediately behind the bomber formation, climb almost vertically several thousand feet, and then loop over into a diving attack, sometimes breaking out through their own contrails. Some Komet pilots preferred to make a high nose attack and then climb away for a high tail attack, while others snaked up and down through the target formation, firing continuously without singling out an individual airplane for attention, then barrelling up through the formation, gaining a few hundred feet of altitude and attacking again in a diving pass.

The first real success of Jagdgesch-

05

wader 400 was achieved on 5th August when three Komets knocked down three P-51B Mustangs from the 352nd Fighter Group escorting a Fortress formation attacking targets in the area of Magdeburg. The destruction of the trio of AAF fighters was described in a report by a crewman of one of the bombers participating in the mission: 'Within two minutes of turning at the IP, I saw puffing vapor trails coming from three Me 163s which were about 35,000 feet high and at nine o'clock to our course.'

'They flew in the direction of our formation then turned left to attack three P-51s which were flying approximately 3,000 feet above and to the left of our formation. The jets dived onto the P-51s, which, at that time, were at about eight o'clock to our formation. The Me 163s were in trail as they swooped down on the P-51s. The attacks were pressed almost to point-blank range, then the German aircraft zoom-climbed into the clear sky above. I saw each of the three P-51s catch fire and dive earthward.' The Komet had drawn first blood, and a further eleven days were to pass before one of the rocket-driven interceptors was itself to fall victim to AAF fighters.

On 16th August P-51 Mustangs of the 359th Fighter Group – the same unit that had recorded the first AAF encounter with the Komet nearly three weeks earlier – were engaged in escorting a B-17 Fortress Wing in the vicinity of Leipzig. Several attacks had been made on the bombers by Me 163Bs without positive results when one of the P-51 pilots, Lieutenant-Colonel John B Murphy, saw a Komet contrail approaching the B-17 boxes from eight o'clock at a distance of approximately two miles.

The Komet climbed to 28,000 feet and, some 400 yards behind the bombers, the pilot cut his rocket motor. Murphy, on the opposite side of the bombers to the Komet and unable to intercept the German fighter before it could make its first firing pass, guessed that the Komet pilot would be attracted by a solitary B-17 straggling some two miles behind the main bomber force, and swung his P-51 towards this tempting target. Although Murphy's P-51 was clocking more than 400mph IAS, and had only two miles to cover, the Komet travelled more than a mile to the main bomber formation, passed it and covered the additional two miles to the straggler before the AAF fighter could reach the B-17.

Fortunately for the straggling bomber, the Komet overshot its target and began to flatten out below the bomber. At an altitude of 23,000 feet and a half-mile beyond the B-17, Murphy opened fire from a distance of 300 yards with fifteen degrees deflection, closing to point-blank range and getting strikes on the tail and portside of the Komet before he overshot and pulled off steeply to the left. Murphy's wingman, Lieutenant Cyril W Jones who had followed him down, came in slightly below the Komet at an angle of ten degrees to starboard and began firing at some 350 yards. The Komet immediately flipped on its back and began a Split-S, but Jones hit the German fighter's canopy with a sixty-degree deflection shot. His P-51 then hit the wash of the Komet and he blacked out, recovering at 14,000 feet.

Lieutenant Jones was only credited with damaging the Komet, but meanwhile, Murphy had seen another Komet circling some 5,000 feet below and to port of his P-51. He peeled off and dived to position himself slightly ahead of his intended victim. The Komet completed two turns of a slightly inclined spiral as the P-51 closed at 400mph IAS in a thirty-degree dive. Murphy opened fire with ten degrees of deflection from 250 yards and closed to thirty-five yards, firing continuously. He stayed inside the Komet's turn for between five and

P-51 Mustangs were the first Allied fighters to tangle with the Komet

VF
WD
WD A
WD C
41377

B-17G Fortresses were the primary Komet target

ten seconds before overshooting, and the 0.5-inch calibre bullets that he had pumped into the rear portside of the German fighter's fuselage had found their mark. From the cockpit aft the whole of the lefthand side of the Komet's fuselage was ripped away by a tremendous explosion, and the Me 163B went down in a fast spiral. This time there was no element of doubt. The AAF had its first confirmed Komet 'kill'. But casualties in combat were the least of Jagdgeschwader 400's worries; attrition totally unrelated to enemy action was the primary cause for concern. The Komet had been committed to battle but was still far from maturity as a weapon.

Meanwhile, a second squadron, 2 Staffel, had been formed within Jagdgeschwader 400 and, under the command of Hauptmann Böhner, had joined combat from Venlo on the Dutch border. However, with tho replacement of Generalleutnant Adolf Galland by Oberst Gordon M Gollob on the special operational staff for jet fighters, changes in the entire Luftwaffe defence concept had been initiated. Gollob, who, from October 1942 until April 1944, had

occupied the position of Jafü 5 (Fighter Leader 5) in the west, and was a member of the Jägerstab (Fighter Staff) within the Ministry of Armament, did not subscribe to Galland's policy of deploying one rocket fighter Staffel at one base. In view of the Luftwaffe's failure to maintain air superiority over the Third Reich, Gollob favoured a concentration of effort, and therefore, at the end of August 1944, the 2 Staffel of JG 400 had joined the 1 Staffel at Brandis, each Staffel then having some fifteen operational Komets and ten to twelve pilots.

The primary task of the two Brandis-based Staffeln, which were eventually to be designated the I Gruppe of JG 400 and commanded by Hauptmann Fulda, (who, oddly enough, was a paratroop captain) was the protection of the Leuna synthetic fuel plants, but these were situated on the outer edge of the Komet's radius of action, and as the Allies quickly realised that the Achilles' Heel of the Komet was its strictly limited endurance, the AAF formations were soon taking pains to avoid Brandis when attacking the Leuna plants, and, in consequence, the Komet Staffeln could make only limited contact with the intruders.

Variations on a theme

The short powered endurance of the Komet had given cause for concern from the moment that it was acknowledged that the fuel consumption of Walter's 'hot' rocket motor was very much greater than that anticipated, and Professor Walter had begun investigating the possibility of introducing an auxiliary cruising chamber. A rocket motor fitted with such a chamber had developed as far as test status during the spring of 1944, and had been installed in two B-series test airplanes, the Me 163B V6 and the Me 163B V18.

The cruising chamber afforded a thrust of 660 pounds, this being additional to the normal full-power thrust rating, and the intention was that the interceptor should take off and climb to operational altitude with both rocket chambers operating at full thrust, the pilot then cutting the main chamber and cruising on the power of the auxiliary chamber alone. Apart from the provision of a fully-retractable tailwheel, situated further forward to allow for the twin vertically-disposed rocket pipes, some revision of the keel line and a shortening of the landing skid, the Me 163B V6 and V18 were externally similar to the standard B-series production airplanes.

On 6th July 1944, Opitz took-off from Peenemünde in the Me 163B V18 for the first climb calibration trials with both rocket chambers functioning. The instrument panel was being photographed automatically at each increment of 1,640 feet in altitude, and everything went according to plan until, just above 13,000 feet, the airplane suddenly began to accelerate. At 14,760 feet the climb rate was increasing at a tremendous rate, and within four seconds the Komet had passed 16,400 feet. Another few seconds and the airplane had exceeded its critical Mach number, forcing Opitz to cut the rocket motor. The Komet immediately went into a steep dive from which Opitz only succeeded in recovering a few feet above the waters of the Baltic. After landing back at Peenemünde, Opitz discovered that almost the entire rudder of the Komet had been ripped away, and it was subsequently ascertained that the test plane had attained a speed of 702mph.

While the testing of the Me 163B V6 and V18 was proceeding at Peenemünde, the Messerschmitt drawing office at Oberammergau, the company's engineering design headquarters supervised by Dr Waldemar Voigt, was finalising a refined version of Alexander Lippisch's basic design, the Me 163C. This was intended from the outset to employ the auxiliary cruising chamber, and while the wings of the new model remained essentially unchanged, a new centre section was introduced which increased overall span and gross area from thirty feet, seven and one third inches and 199.132 square feet to thirty-two feet, one and seven eighths inches and 219.583 square feet respectively. This wing was married to an enlarged fuselage of improved fineness ratio which housed the pilot in a pressurised cockpit enclosed by a blister-type all-round vision canopy. The T-Stoff and C-Stoff tankage was increased, and the armament, which could comprise wither two 20mm MG 151 or two 30mm MK 108 cannon, was transferred from the wing roots to the fuselage, empty equipped weight rising from 4,200 to 4,850 pounds and maximum loaded weight from 9,500 to 11,684 pounds.

The proposed production model, the Me 163C-la, was expected to offer a very similar speed performance to that of the B-series Komet, ranging from 515mph at sea level to 596mph between 13,000 and 40,000 feet, but whereas the service ceiling of the Me 163B was restricted to 39,500 feet, it was calculated that the Me 163C would be capable of reaching 52,000 feet, while the maximum full-power endurance after climbing to 32,810 feet was extended from 2.5 to 6.5 minutes. The twin-chamber rocket motor for the Me 163C, the HWK 509C-1, provided a maximum thrust of 4,410 pounds, 3,750 pounds of this being afforded by the main chamber and the remaining 660 pounds by the auxiliary chamber. Plans for the large-scale production of the C-series Komet were formulated, but these were to be abandoned in favour of a derivative of a parallel development of the design, the Me 163D, and only three Me 163C prototypes were built.

Apart from the unpredictable nature of its rocket motor and its strictly limited endurance, the Komet suffered another serious shortcoming; once it had landed after a sortie it was immobile. Incapable of manoeuvering on its landing skid, it had to await the arrival of a Scheuschlepper tractor, then being raised on to its take-off dolly by means of inflatable bags inserted beneath the wings so that it could be towed to dispersal, or lifted by a special caterpillar-tracked trailer equipped with hydraulically-operated arms. Lack of mobility on the ground suggested that the bases from which the Komet was flown could well be cluttered with immobile interceptors awaiting retrieval and would therefore be extremely vulnerable to the attentions of any strafing enemy airplanes that happened to be in the vicinity.

This particular shortcoming was appreciated some considerable time before the Komet achieved operational status, and work had begun on the Me 163D which, apart from an entirely redesigned and enlarged fuselage, supplanted the take-off dolly and landing-skid arrangement with a more orthodox fully-retractable tricycle undercarriage. The Me 163D retained the B-series wing which, externally at least, remained virtually unchanged, but the structure was suitably modified to permit the insertion of C-Stoff tanks of substantially increased capacity, each wing housing a twenty-five US gallon tank in the leading edge and a sixty-five US gallon tank behind the mainspar.

A further C-Stoff tank of forty-two US gallon capacity was inserted in the fuselage immediately forward of the wing auxiliary spar attachment points, this being intended to supply the rocket motor during the acceleration phase. The T-Stoff was accommodated by a 257 US gallon tank behind the cockpit bulkhead, a thirty-four US gallon tank between the main and auxiliary spar attachment points, and a 132 US gallon tank immediately aft of the latter. A similar HWK 509C-1 twin-chamber rocket motor to that of the C-series was proposed, and all three members of the hydraulically-operated tricycle undercarriage had levered-suspension legs, the nosewheel retracting aft into a well

beneath the pilot's seat and the main members retracting vertically upwards into the fuselage.

A D-series prototype, the Me 163D V1, had been completed in the late spring of 1944, performing satisfactory towed tests with the tricycle undercarriage fixed in the extended position However, by this time, the Air Ministry had concluded that Messerschmitt possessed insufficient engineering manpower to devote adequate attention to the Me 163D in view of the extent of the company's other development work, and instructions had been issued to turn the entire project over to the Junkers organisation at Dessau. Professor Heinrich Hertel, who had joined Junkers in March 1939 after some years as Heinkel's Technical Director and Chief of Development, considered some aspects of the Me 163D irrational and others impracticable from the production viewpoint, and had immediately begun to re-work the design. However, the urgency attached by the Luftwaffe

Above **and *right*: The Me 163B V6 begins a 'sharp start'. This aircraft served as a prototype for the Me 163C with auxiliary rocket cruise chamber**

General Staff and, in turn, by the Technical Department of the Air Ministry, to making ready this more advanced rocket-driven interceptor for the assembly lines placed some restriction on the extent of the redesign that could be undertaken at Dessau.

Apart from the replacement of the fixed wing slots by automatic slots and an increase in the landing flap area, the principal changes introduced by Junkers were confined to the fuselage and were in part the result of a decision to embody cabin pressurisation. The decking immediately aft of the cockpit was cut down, and the pilot was provided with a jettisonable blown hood of sandwich-type construction. The fuselage was a duralumin, semi-monocoque built in three sections. The forward section, which accommodated the pressurised cockpit, nosewheel well, generator and radio equipment, was riveted to the main section housing the three T-Stoff and one C-Stoff tanks, the ammunition tanks, and the main undercarriage wells. The aft section, enclosing the feedlines, combustion chambers and their support tube, were detachable for inspection and maintenance of the rocket motor. The HWK 509C rocket installation was similar to that of the Me 163C but the main support tube between the combustion chambers and the thrust spider was shortened by about a foot.

The armour nose cone of the earlier Komets was not fitted, but the pilot was adequately protected with a 20mm armour segment covering his legs and lower trunk, two 12mm segments overlapping to cover the upper portion of his body, and a 100mm armourglass windscreen. A small segment of 12mm armour above the glass screen afforded protection against frontal and downward attack, and the pilot's back was protected by a 20mm 'head-and-shoulder' plate butt-jointed to a 12mm rear slab.

Armament consisted of a pair of 30mm MK 108 cannon, one in each wing root, with 150 shells per gun in tanks mounted above the mainwheel wells. Radio equipment comprised the usual FuG 25a set for IFF (Identification Friend-Foe) and FuG 16zy for plane-to-plane and plane-to-ground communication, plus FuG 16zvg for direction finding. It was planned, however, to replace the two last-mentioned sets with FuG 15 combining frequency- and amplitude-modulated communications and direction-finding in the one set.

In view of the amount of redesign undertaken by Junkers, the Me 163D was redesignated Ju 248, and the first prototype, the Ju 248 V1, was com-

All that remained of the rudder of the Me 163B V18 after a test flight

pleted at Dessau early in August 1944. Initial handling trials, using the machine as a glider, were completed during the course of the month, the prototype being towed into the air behind a Ju 188 bomber, and the undercarriage being fixed in the extended position. By September, when the HWK 509C rocket motor had been installed and the first powered flight trials begun, plans had been formulated – and accepted – by the Air Ministry for large-scale manufacture of the Junkers-developed interceptor. But at this stage the Air Ministry insisted that the designation 'Ju 248' be discarded in favour of 'Me 263'. They decided that the aircraft should remain essentially a product of the Messerschmitt AG, and the order stated that the change was 'in accordance with established procedure'.

At the same time, it was proposed that the HWK 509C should be replaced at the earliest possible opportunity by another rocket motor, the BMW 708 which, using S-Stoff (ninety to ninety-seven per cent nitric acid and three to ten per cent sulphuric acid) and R-Stoff, or 'Tonka', (fifty-seven per cent crude oxide monoxylidene and forty-three per cent tri-ethylamine), was expected to give a maximum thrust of 5,510 pounds. Shortly afterwards, at a meeting of the Entwicklungs Hauptkommission (Chief Development Commission) held in Berlin on 22nd December 1944, the decision was taken to expedite development of the Me 263 by all possible means, and that tooling should be given the highest possible priority. This was hardly a realistic decision in view of the rapidity with which the military situation was deteriorating.

By the summer of 1944, Germany was not alone in pursuing development based on Lippisch's original rocket-driven interceptor design, for, on the other side of the world, the Japanese, too, were actively engaged in evolving a rocket-propelled fighter based broadly on the design of the Komet. Under the Nippon-German Technical Exchange Agreement, the Japanese military and naval attachés in Berlin had been informed of German progress in the development of rocket-driven interceptor fighters in the autumn of 1943, and the attachés of both services, together with their staffs, had visited Bad Zwischenahn soon after EK 16 had been transferred to this field from Peenemünde.

The Japanese, who were not unaware of the development in the USA of the B-29 Superfortress and the AAF's intentions concerning the operational use to which this mighty weapon was to be put, were enthralled by the Komet. Although the unstable nature of the fuels that the rocket motor used, and its unpredictable behaviour, were patiently explained to the delegation, the Japanese, in whom fanaticism and fatalism went far deeper than in their German hosts, considered the dangers to be of little consequence. They needed a fast-climbing, high-speed target defence interceptor, and they felt that here was the ideal weapon with which to combat and defeat the American bombing offensive they knew must inevitably begin sooner or later.

Time was important to the Japanese and negotiations began immediately for the acquisition of manufacturing licences for both the Komet airframe and its HWK 509A rocket motor, the licence for the latter alone costing twenty million Reichsmarks. Under the agreement, Germany was to supply the Japanese government with complete blueprints and manufacturing data for the Me 163B and its power plant, one complete airframe, two sets of sub-assemblies and components, and three complete HWK 509A rocket motors by 1st March 1944. Furthermore, the German Air Ministry was to keep the Japanese joint-service mission in Berlin apprised of all improvements and developments so that these could be embodied by

Rauche
Sand

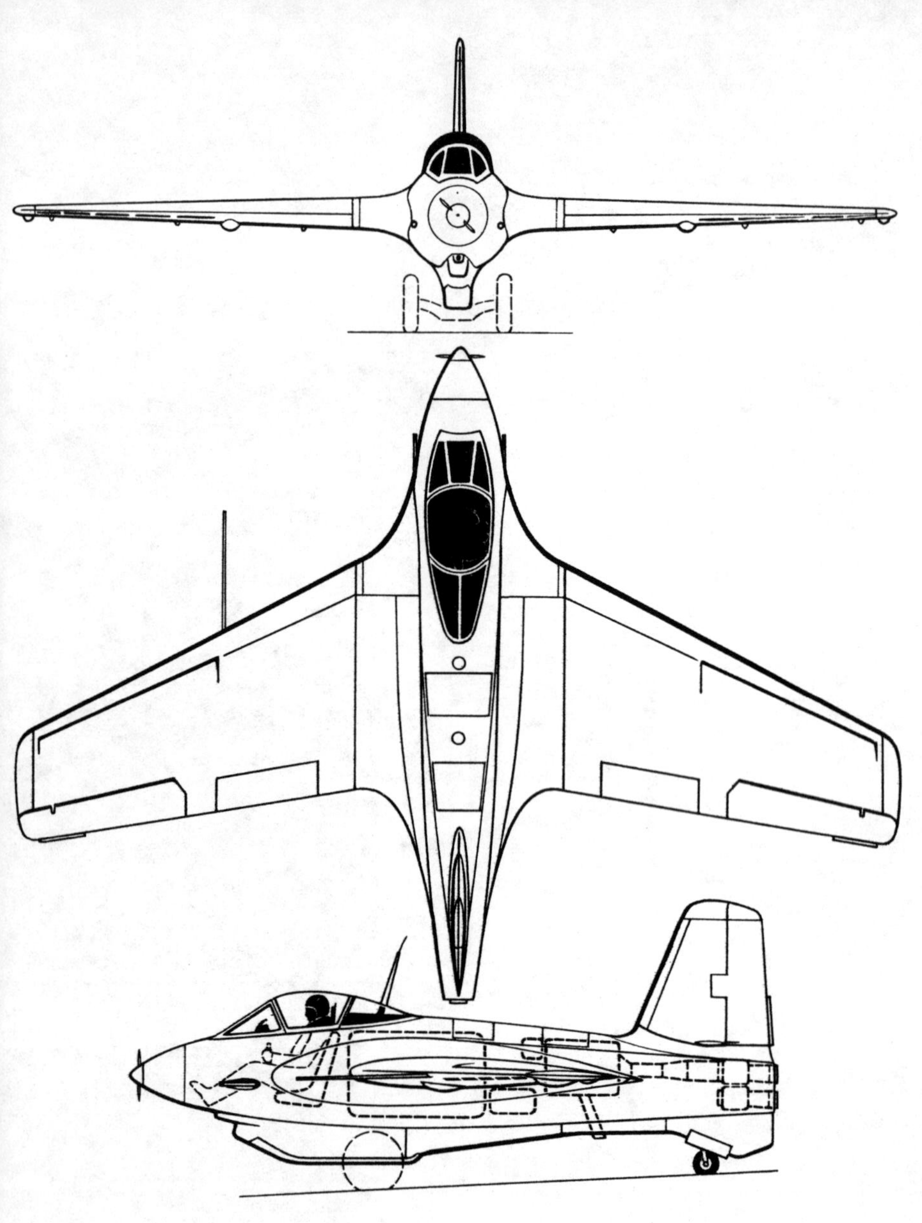

The Me 163C-1a. This aircraft represented a major redesign of Lippisch's original interceptor, embodying a rocket motor with an auxiliary cruise chamber, increased fuel capacity, and cabin pressurization. But take-off and landing methods remained unchanged and, in consequence, it was overtaken by the Me 163D

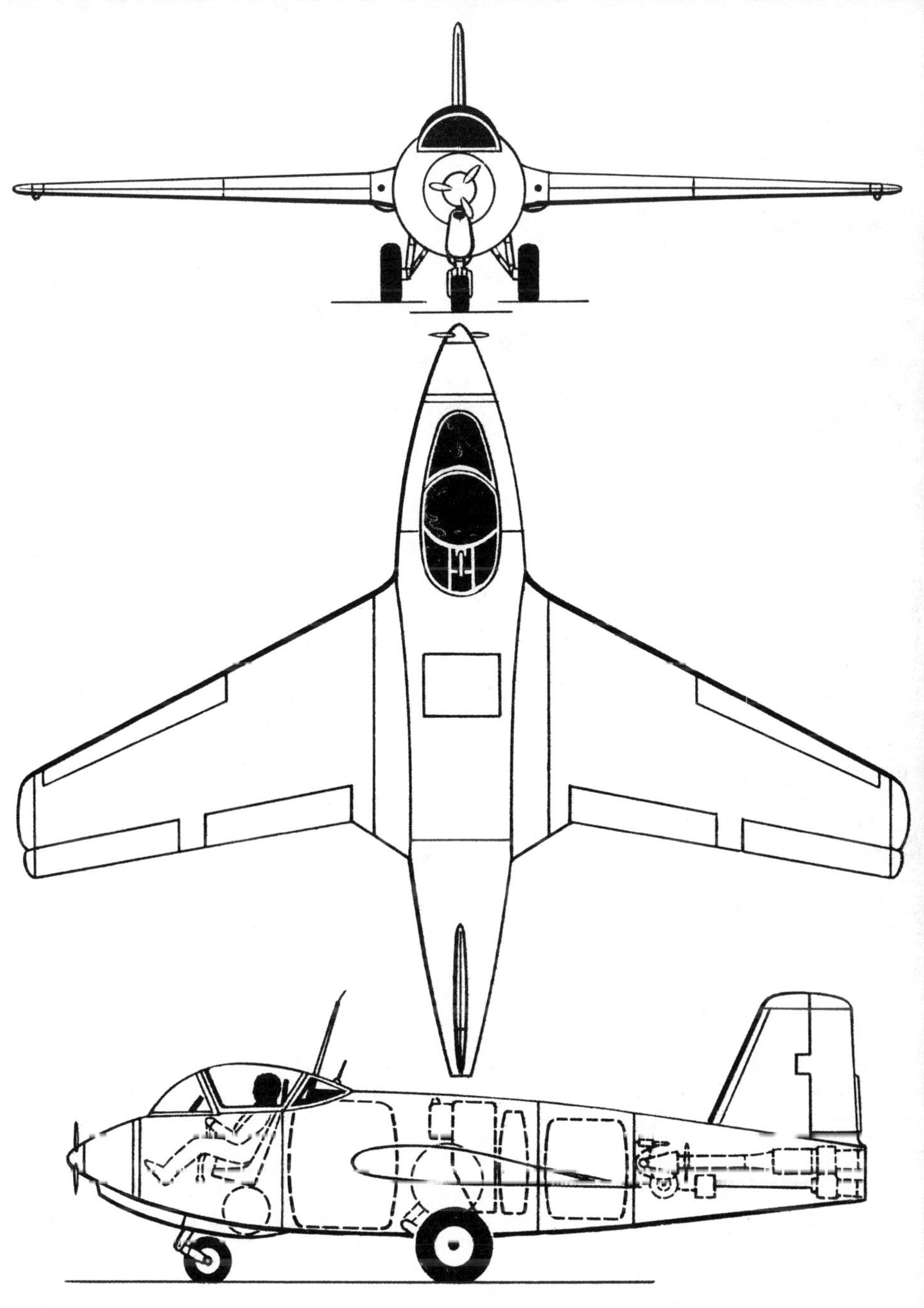

Originally known as the Ju 248 and subsequently redesigned Me 263, this interceptor was a Junkers derivative of the Me 163D but was too late to attain production. However, it provided a basis for postwar Soviet work on rocket-propelled interceptors developed by Mikoyan and Gurevich

The Me 263, alias Ju 248, was the last development of the Komet to be built

Japanese production models. The Japanese were also to be permitted to study German manufacturing processes for both airframe and power plant, and facilities were to be afforded the Japanese joint-service mission to enable it to study Luftwaffe operating techniques for the rocket-propelled interceptor as these evolved.

Unforseen delays and the loss of a submarine conspired to prevent Germay from fulfilling many of the terms of this agreement. Full manufacturing data for the HWK 509A rocket, together with a complete example of this power plant, reached Japan by submarine in the early summer, but a second submarine carrying the example of the Me 163B, as well as the necessary blueprints for its licence manufacture, disappeared and was presumed sunk by enemy action en route from Germany. This left the Japanese with little more than a simple instructional manual on the Komet brought from Germany by a member of the naval mission, Eiichi Iwaya.

The B-29 Superfortress had now appeared over the Japanese home islands, having bombed the steel mills at Yawata on 15th June. The target had suffered little damage, and the initial B-29 attacks were no more than pin-pricks, but the writing on the wall was plainly visible; the AAF offensive was building up and Japan had to be ready with an antidote.

Both services agreed that insufficient time was available to permit them to await submarine delivery from Germany of more substantial material for the Komet airframe. In any case, the chances of a submarine successfully completing the hazardous journey half way around the world at the stage the war had now reached were remote. The decision was thus taken by the Japanese to design with all possible speed an airframe to take a Japanese production version of the HWK 509A rocket motor as a joint-service project. It was at this point, however, that a difference of opinion arose between the army and the navy. Whereas the latter favoured a design following as closely as possible that of the Me 163B because of its proven aerodynamic qualities, the Army Air Headquarters Staff demurred, believing that little time would be lost by complete redesign. However, the navy wielded sufficient influence in government circles to ensure that the 19-Shi (indicating the nineteenth year of the Showa régime – 1944) requirement formulated for a joint-service, rocket-driven, target-defence interceptor stipulated that the design adhered as closely as possible to that of the Komet.

The task of designing and building the airplane was assigned to the Mitsubishi Jukogyo KK, the designation J8M1 being allocated to the naval model and Ki 200 to the version intended for the army. While ostensibly accepting the governmental directive, the army secretly ignored it, and the Army Aerotechnical Research Institute (Rikugun Kokugijitsu Kenkyujo) eventually initiated a major redesign which made good what it considered to be shortcomings in the German design. Meanwhile, in Yokosuka, the 1st Naval Air Technical Arsenal (Dai-Ichi Kaigun Koku Gijitsusho), in collaboration with Mitsubishi, had begun modification of the Walter HWK 509A rocket motor to suit it for Japanese manufacturing techniques.

Design of the airframe by Mitsubishi's team led by Kiro Takahashi and Tetsuro Hikida progressed quickly. The initial mock-up was completed in September and, after minor modifications and changes which occupied three weeks, was inspected and approved by both services, although the army's attitude to the whole project remained unchanged.

At the same time, work was progressing in the Arsenal at Yokosuka on a full-scale wooden glider version of the interceptor under the supervision of Hidemasa Kimura. He had led the team responsible for the design of the Tachikawa-built A-2600 long-range airplane which, originally sponsored by the Asahi Press, had created a new international closed-circuit distance record of 10,212 miles only a few weeks before. The glider, which was designated MXY8 and named Akigusa (Autumn Grass), had two purposes: to provide experience in the handling characteristics of an airplane configuration with which the Japanese were unfamiliar, and to provide a means of expediting the training of the pilots eventually to be assigned to the rocket-driven fighter.

The MXY-8 Akigusa was completed in December, and flown from the Hyakurigahara Airfield by Lieutenant-Commander Toyohiko Inuzuka after being towed from the ground by a Kyushu K10W1. Toyohiko found that the Akigusa emulated the Komet's outstanding handling characteristics in gliding flight, and two further prototypes were completed, one of these being delivered to the Army Aerotechnical Research Institute. Production of a version of the Akigusa equipped with water ballast tanks to simulate more closely the characteristics of the powered airplane was begun by the Maeda Aircraft Institute on behalf of the navy, and by the Yokoi Koku KK for the army, the series model being designated Ku-13.

The J8M1 (alias Ki202) had meanwhile received the appellation of Shusui, or 'Sword Wind', and work was proceeding rapidly at Nagoya on twelve prototypes. Although possessing a close superficial resemblance to the Komet on which it was based, the Shusui differed greatly in detail. Fuel tankage was much the same as that of the Me 163B, totalling 306 US gallons of T-Stoff and 142 US gallons of C-Stoff which were fed into the combustion chamber at a ratio of 10 to 3.6 and the arrangement of the tanks followed a similar pattern. The overall dimensions differed marginally: the span of the wing was increased by a few inches to thirty-one feet two inches, although its gross area was reduced to 190.84 square feet, and a slightly longer nose cone (which lacked the wind-driven generator airscrew of the Komet) increased length to nineteen feet, ten and a quarter inches.

The most marked difference was to be found in the empty equipped and maximum loaded weights, which, at

3,318 and 8,598 pounds repectively, were 880-900 pounds less than those of the Me 163B. This did not reflect any attempt to achieve a dramatically lighter structure, but simply the lack of importance attached to armour protection for the pilot, coupled with reduced ammunition capacity. Whereas the Komet's 'pneumatic hammers' – as the MK 108 cannon were dubbed – were each provided with sixty rounds, provision was made for only fifty rounds for each of the similar-calibre weapons proposed for the Shusui. The prime directive had been that there should be as few differences as possible between the versions of the Shusui for the two services, and apart from some minor equipment items, it was only in the type of gun specified for installation that the two models differed.

The J8M1 for the navy was to have two Type 5 cannon of 30mm calibre and each weighing 154 pounds, whereas the K200 for the army was intended to receive two 97-pound Ho 105 cannon, also of 30mm calibre. The effective range of both navy and army weapons was 985 yards, but the former had a slightly higher muzzle velocity and a lower rate of fire, these being 2,460 feet per second and 400 rounds per minute as compared with 2,350 feet per second and 450 rounds per minute offered by the army cannon. By comparison with the Japanese guns, the German MK 108 employed by the Komet weighed 128 pounds and fired 650 rounds per minute, but its muzzle velocity was only 1,705 feet per second.

The Japanese derivative of the HWK 509A rocket motor, the Toko Ro.2 (KR10), delivered somewhat less thrust than did its German prototype, affording 3,310 pounds, and although the Shusui was almost ten per cent lighter than the Komet in its fully-loaded condition, it was evidently calculated by Takahashi and Hikida that the lower weight would not fully compensate for the reduced thrust, as estimated performance figures included climbing times of two minutes and sixteen seconds to 19,685 feet, three minutes and thirty seconds to 32,810 feet, and three minutes and fifty seconds to the maximum ceiling of 39,370 feet. Maximum attainable speed was estimated at 559mph at 32,800 feet.

The Army Air Headquarters, considering that it has saved face by tacitly ignoring the directive concerning commonality between the rocket-driven, target-defence interceptors to be built for the two services, initiated its own redesign of the Ki200 at the Army Aerotechnical Research Institute on 1st March 1945, calling it the Ki202 Shusui-Kai ('Sword Wind – Modified'). The Ki202 was intended to afford a substantial improvement on the five and a half minutes' powered endurance envisaged for the Shusui, and it was considered the priority army interceptor project for service from 1946 onwards. In the event, Ki202 design was still incomplete when the Pacific War ended, and no metal had been cut on a prototype.

The first prototype of the Shusui, completed to naval J8M1 standards but naturally possessing no operational equipment, was rolled out of Mitsubishi's Number One Plant in Nagoya during the second week of June 1945, barely eleven months after the formulation of the 19-Shi requirement to which it has been built. By this time, pilots of both services had begun training courses on the similarly-configured Ku53 glider. Mitsubishi, with Fuji Hikoki and Nissan Jidosha acting as sub-contractors, was well advanced with tooling for the large-scale production of two versions of the Shusui for the navy, the J8M1 and the J8M2. The latter model differed in having armament reduced to a single Type 5 cannon and a modest increase in fuel tankage.

The first prototype Shusui was transferred from Nagoya to Yokosuka where, after a series of tethered trials with the Toko Ro.2 rocket motor running, it was prepared for its initial

Above: **The MXY-8 Akigusa glider, intended for the training of pilots for the Japanese version of the Komet, the J8M1 Shusui (below)**

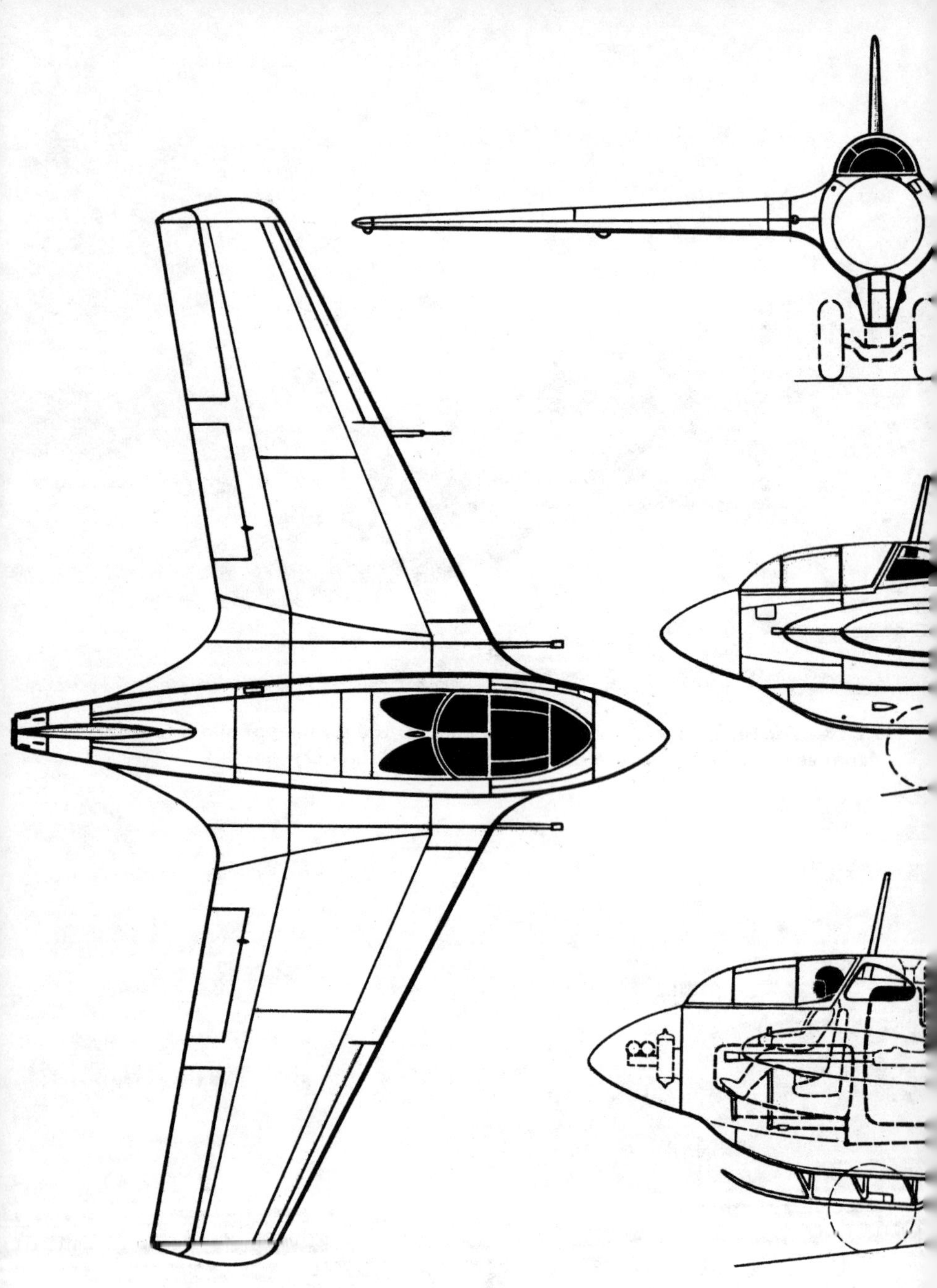

The Mitsubishi J8M1 Shusui rocket interceptor, based broadly on the design of the Me 163B Komet. It had become a priority development programme as the Pacific War drew to a close. It was also intended for use by the army as the Ki 200, but this service had its own ideas on rocket-powered interceptors

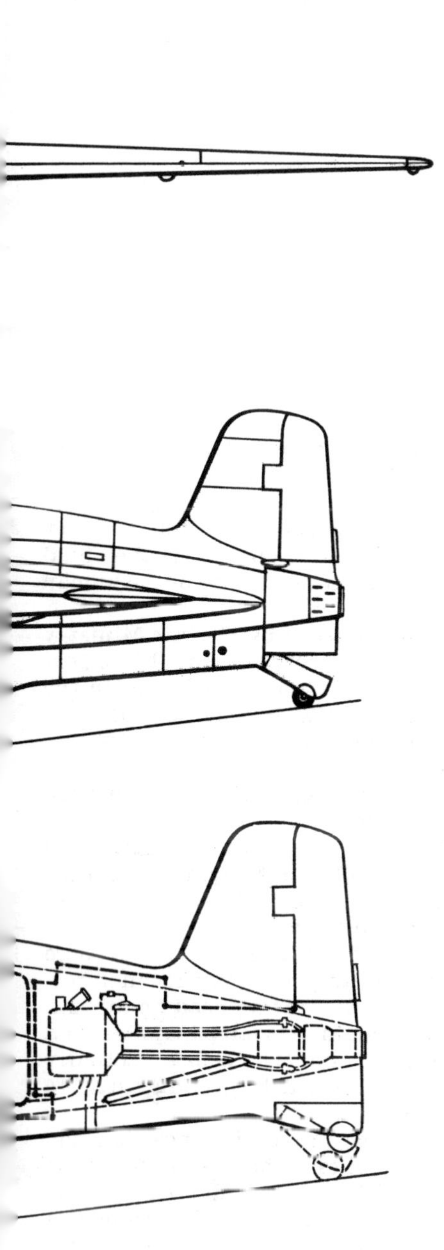

flight test. With half-filled tanks, this Germano-Nipponese rocket-driven interceptor took-off on its first flight on 7th July 1945. The pilot, Toyohiko Inuzuka, successfully jettisoned the undercarriage dolly, gathered speed rapidly, and then pulled up the nose of the Shusui in a forty-five degree climb. Almost immediately, at 1,300 feet, the rocket motor failed, the Shusui stalled, and then dived vertically into the ground and the pilot was killed. Several other Shusui prototypes were already being prepared for participation in the test programme, but further trials were halted pending the results of a hurried investigation of the accident.

Only a year had elapsed since the fleet submarine I-29 arrived in Japan with the pattern HWK 509A rocket motor, but in that short time the Japanese copy of this power plant had completed a number of extremely successful bench runs at full power, and there was no obvious reason for its failure. Navy and Mitsubishi technicians could only conclude that the failure of the rocket had resulted from activation of the automatic cut-out device by an air lock in a fuel feedline, this presumably having been caused by the sudden shifting of the fuel in the partly-filled tanks when Inuzuka began his climb. Permission to continue the flight test programme was withheld pending modification of the fuel pumps, the sixth and seventh Shusui prototypes, which were about to leave the assembly line, being selected to test the modified Ro.2 rocket motor.

Preparations for the full-scale production of the Shusui were continued, component manufacture had begun, and on the morning of 15th August, with the flight testing of the Shusui scheduled to be resumed in a few days, the design of the improved J8M2 model was finalised. However, that morning was to be remembered for an event of far greater importance – an Imperial proclamation announced Japan's unconditional surrender.

The exotic and the fantastic

By the spring of 1944 it was becoming increasingly obvious to the Luftwaffe General Staff that the steadily escalating daylight offensive being mounted by the Allied Air Force against the industry of the Third Reich could no longer be countered solely by orthodox means. Indeed, so serious was the situation that careful consideration had to be given the unorthodox, and there was no shortage of highly ingenious schemes for intercepting and destroying the intruding bomber formations. Few withstood more than a cursory examination of their practicability, but those of which development was pursued were certainly exotic and, for originality of concept, even fantastic.

At the beginning of the previous year, AAF B-17 Fortress formations had begun to penetrate German air space, flying in tight combat boxes to give maximum defensive power. Early battle experience had indicated that the frontal area of a Focke-Wulf 190's radial air-cooled engine – some seventeen square feet – provided a target capable of being hit by the average B-17 gunner at a range of more than 1,000 yards. It was axiomatic that the only means by which this target could be substantially reduced was the discarding of the bulky piston engine, and rocket power was seen by many as the logical solution to this problem. The reduction in frontal area rendered possible by the use of a rocket motor was being exploited to some degree by the Komet, but the design of this interceptor made no attempt to carry this reduction down to the final limiting factor – the size of the human frame.

With the issue by the Air Ministry of a requirement for a small inexpensive target-defence interceptor in the spring of 1944, it was logical that most of the contenders for production contracts should be rocket-powered, and equally logical that, for the same reasons prompting John K Northrop when formulating the configuration of the XP-79 some eighteen months earlier, several of these should propose a prone position for their pilot, thus reducing frontal area to the bare minimum and resulting in an interceptor that, in a head-on attack, would remain virtually invisible to a bomber's gunners before actually opening fire with its large calibre cannon.

While the prone pilot position had its adherents, who declaimed that results of tests conducted by the DVL (German Aviation Experimental Establishment) from the late 'thirties offered proof positive of the efficacy of this unorthodox style of accommodation, the Air Ministry possessed its hard core of traditionalists which had sufficient difficulty in accepting the rocket motor as a viable means of propelling a fighter without taxing its imagination still further by coupling so radical a prime mover with so innovatory a means of housing the pilot. It was hardly surprising therefore, that the favoured contender for priority development when the Air Ministry completed its evaluation of the competing proposals in the autumn of 1944 was Heinkel's Project 1077, which, referred to by its cover-name of 'Julia', was offered with both prone and orthodox pilot accommodation.

Alexander Lippisch had in fact considered the possibilities of a prone position for the pilot during the summer of 1941, one of the project studies undertaken by Department 'L' at Augsburg-Haunstetten that were to lead to the definitive Komet configuration, the P 01-117, embodying this feature. But although the DVL had already ascertained that whereas the average pilot in the normal sitting posture usually blacked-out at pressures between four and five times that of gravity, the onset of black-out could be delayed to as much as ten or eleven-g with the pilot lying prone, the general consensus of opinion was that the pilot of a fighter would enjoy insufficient field of vision from this 'abnormal' recumbent position.

The DVL had initiated a careful study during the 'thirties of methods enabling a pilot to withstand high *g* values, and in 1937 the Flight Technical Study Group of the Berlin-Charlottenburg Technical High School had built a small prone-pilot airplane, the Berlin B 9, to participate in the research programme. The B 9, which was powered by two 105 hp Hirth HM 500 air-cooled engines, was extensively flown at the Rechlin test centre and elsewhere, but primary interest was centred on ascertaining the practicability of the prone position for dive-bomber pilots who were called upon to withstand inordinately high *g* values during pull-outs. Thus it was not until the necessity arose to develop target-defence interceptors offering the minimum frontal area to opposing gunners that serious consideration was given to the possibility that fighter pilots would adopt the prone position.

The choice of the Heinkel P 1077 Julia as the winning contender in the target-defence interceptor programme was somewhat surprising in view of the radical nature of its concept (reminiscent of that submitted to the Air Ministry five years earlier by Wernher von Braun), the Julia being intended to take off vertically from guide rails with the aid of a battery of booster rockets and to land on skids after completion of its mission. The runner-up, the Junkers EF 127 which rejoiced under the cover name of 'Dolly' and had been conceived in collaboration with the DFS (German Research Institute for Gliding Flight), which, indirectly, had fathered the Komet, was somewhat more 'conventional' in that it was intended to take off in orthodox fashion with the aid of a jettisonable three-wheel trolley and, like the Julia II, offered the pilot a normal seat.

The Air Ministry issued instructions for development of both the P 1077 Julia and the EF 127 Dolly to proceed, the latter as a back-up programme to safeguard against the more radical Heinkel project proving unacceptable, and work proceeded in parallel with another emergency fighter programme, the so-called Volksjäger, or 'People's Fighter'. The Volksjäger was essentially similar in concept to the Air Ministry's target defence interceptor in that it envisaged a simple, inexpensive combat airplane suitable for quantity production by semi-skilled and unskilled labour, and using, insofar as was feasible, readily-available materials, but in place of the rocket motor a single turbojet was to be employed. The Volksjäger was allegedly the brainchild of Party Leader Otto Saur who headed the Jägerstab or Fighter

A Berlin B9 research aircraft, in use in the first prone-pilot experiments. The position was adopted as a means of reducing the frontal area and the target that it offered B-17 gunners

Staff that had been formed within the War Ministry on 1st March 1944, and was the energetic protégé of Albert Speer, the Minister of Armaments. Although vehement opposition to the Volksjäger was to be voiced by Adolf Galland, the General der Jagdflieger, and the Technical Department of the Air Ministry, Saur possessed sufficient political influence to force the project through, and the 'People's Fighter' was eventually to take precedence over the rocket-powered target-defence interceptor.

The P 1077 Julia and the EF 127 Dolly were to be joined in the programme by an outsider, the Bachem BP 20 Natter (Adder), which differed from the Heinkel and Junkers projects in being *semi-expendable*. The Natter represented a halfway house between interceptor and missile, and when submitted as a contender in the target-defence interceptor programme had been rejected by the Air Ministry out of hand. The Natter project, tendered by Erich Bachem, had been uninvited and had also been submitted for consideration through abnormal channels. Bachem enlisted the aid of Adolf Galland who had himself passed the proposal to the Air Ministry with his recommendation that it be developed. This unorthodox procedure had incensed the Air Ministry's Technical Department which considered such an approach a supreme example of meddling on the part of the General der Jagdflieger. In defence of the Ministry, however, it should be stated that Bachem's project did not meet the demands of the requirement, which did not envisage partial loss of the interceptor after each mission.

Convinced of the viability of his proposals and refusing to accept defeat in this fashion, Bachem promptly applied for and was granted an interview with no less a personage than Heinrich Himmler. Himmler displayed immediate interest in the Natter, promised his full support, and within twenty-four hours Bachem was informed by the Technical Department that it had reconsidered its earlier rejection of his proposals which would now receive the highest development priority, the Natter being allocated the official designation 'Ba 349'.

It was proposed to power all three target-defence interceptors by the Walter HWK 509C rocket motor with auxiliary cruising chamber, the main chamber of which afforded 3,750 pounds of thrust and the auxiliary chamber a further 660 pounds. To enable it to take off almost vertically from guide rails, the P 1077 Julia was to be fitted with four solid-fuel Schmidding 533 booster rockets each providing 2,205 pounds of thrust for twelve seconds. The skids and strengthened wingtips were to run in the guide-rails of a near-vertical ramp which was to be pivoted at its base to enable the aircraft to be 'loaded' in the horizontal position. The Schmidding booster rockets were intended to be jettisoned automatically on burn-out, and it was calculated that the initial acceleration would not exceed 2.06 g, but the possibility of the pilot blacking-out was to be safeguarded against by pre-setting the control surfaces for the required flights path while the Julia was still on the ramp. A three-axis autopilot ground-controlled by radio link assumed guidance of the interceptor automatically as soon as the booster rockets were jettisoned. The pilot was to override the autopilot control some one or two miles from the bomber formation that he was to attack.

The Julia was an extremely simple shoulder-wing monoplane spanning only 15ft 1in and possessing an overall length of 22ft 5½in. Its gross wing area was a mere 77.5 square feet, and the prone-pilot Julia I with a flying weight of 3,957 pounds at take-off (ie, after the booster rockets had been jettisoned) had a wing loading of fifty-one pounds per square foot, the loading of the Julia II, which, with the pilot seated in conventional fashion had a flying weight of 4,056 pounds,

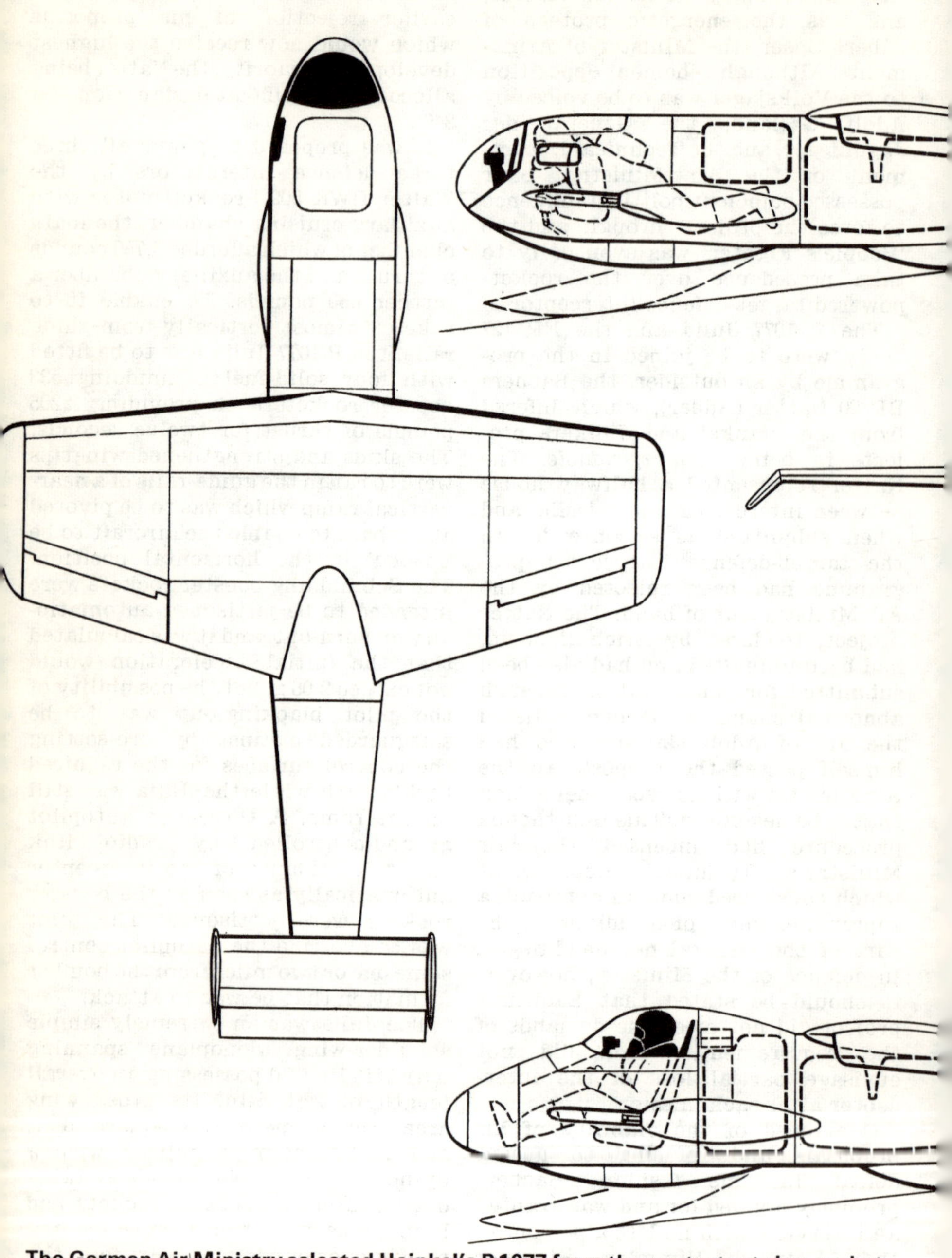

The German Air Ministry selected Heinkel's P 1077 from the contestants in a rocket-driven target-defence interceptor competition. It was allocated the cover name 'Julia', and two versions were proposed, the Julia I with a prone pilot and the Julia II with normal pilot accommodation

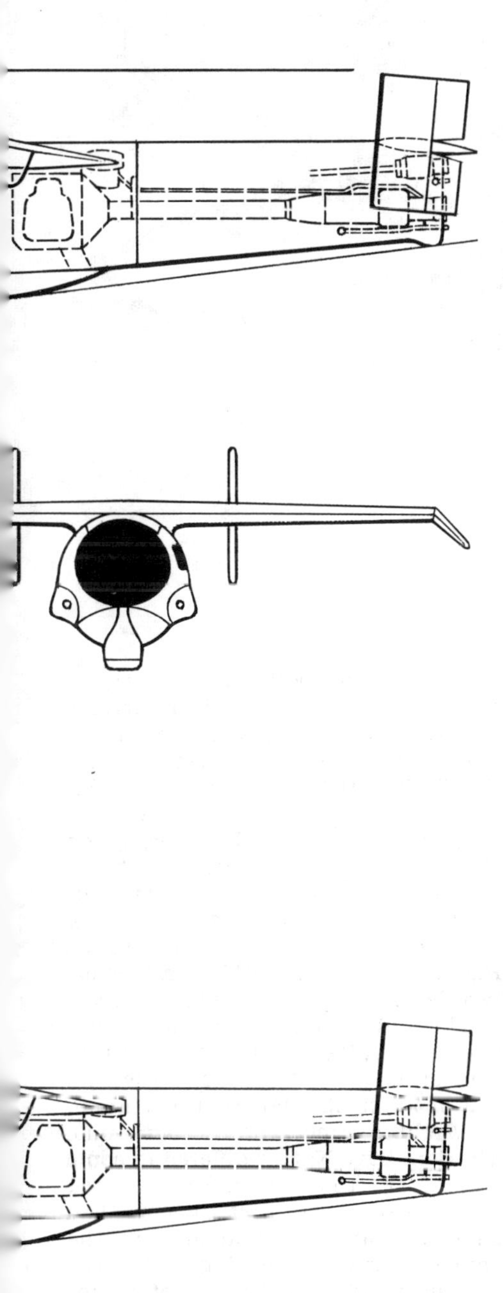

being slightly higher. Of the loaded weight 490 pounds were C-Stoff and 1,550 were T-Stoff, and thus with fuel and ammunition expended, the gliding return to base was to be made at a weight of around 1,600 pounds, wing loading then being marginally more than twenty pounds per square foot. The landing itself was to be made on tandem skids, the forward portion of the skid beneath the cockpit was extended to absorb the initial touch-down impact, and both skids carried oleo shock-absorbers.

Instrumentation and equipment were spartan, but a normal reflector sight was provided. Armament comprised two 30mm MK 108 cannon, mounted semi-externally on the side of the forward fuselage and provided with sixty rounds per gun, which fired at an angle of plus 3.5 degrees from the horizontal. Performance calculations indicated a maximum level speed of 608mph at 16,400 feet and an initial climb rate of 39,400 feet per minute; an altitude of 16,400 feet was reached in thirty-one seconds and 49,000 feet in seventy-two seconds. Range on the thrust of the cruising chamber was about forty miles at 495mph.

As some doubt existed regarding the wisdom of adopting a ramp to enable the Julia to take-off semi-vertically, an alternative arrangement was offerred by Heinkel which permitted the Julia to take-off in orthodox fashion. This involved the use of a three-wheel jettisonable trolley very similar to that proposed for the competitive Junkers EF 127 Dolly, and it was estimated that by retaining the quartet of Schmidding booster rockets, the Julia would lift off within 380 yards.

Carrying a similar armament to that of the Julia, the EF 127 Dolly was a somewhat larger airplane, its mid-positioned wing spanned 21ft 9¾in and had an area of 95.8 square feet. More orthodox in appearance than that of the Julia, the fuselage was of circular section and 24ft 5½in long, and provided somewhat more fuel

Artist's impression of the P1077 Julia I, the prototypes of which were scrapped

capacity, a 1,100-pound load of C-Stoff being coupled with 2,400 pounds of T-Stoff. Take-off was to be assisted by four Schmidding 563 booster rockets which, attached beneath the wing roots, would each give 1,100 pounds thrust for six seconds, but it was estimated that without the boosters the Dolly would be capable of taking off within 400 yards at its normal take-off weight of 6,140 pounds. Unlike the Julia, the Dolly was intended to be operated in orthodox fashion from take-off to landing, the latter being effected on a long, retractable skid mounted centrally beneath the fuselage. The estimated sea level rate of climb was 26,200 feet per minute, anticipated maximum speeds 630mph at sea level and 560mph at 36,090 feet, and range on the power of the auxiliary cruising chamber at 435mph was expected to be sixty-seven miles at 16,400 feet and sixty-one miles at 32,800 feet.

If Julia and Dolly were exotic in concept, they appeared relatively conventional by comparison with the Erich Bachem's Ba 349 Natter. Once the Technical Department of the Air Ministry had as a result of the pressure applied by Himmler, given the go-ahead for work to begin officially on the Natter project, Bachem was joined at a small factory that he had acquired at Waldsee in the Black Forest by H. Bethbeder, formerly a Technical Director of the Dornier-Werke, and an engineer named Grassow from the Walter-Werke at Kiel. From August 1944 the Natter came within the orbit of the Jägernotprogramm, or Fighter Emergency Programme. The definitive Natter differed in some respects to that originally proposed by Bachem. The first scheme had envisaged an initial attack on the bomber formation during which the Natter would fire a battery of rocket missiles. The pilot would then use the remaining kinetic energy to gain sufficient height for a ramming attack to be performed from a dive. Immediately before impact it was proposed that the pilot would eject himself from the cockpit of the Natter, activation of the ejector seat triggering explosive bolts which would detach the aft fuselage housing the rocket motor. A parachute would then be deployed to lower this to the ground for recovery and re-use.

Bethbeder concluded that the cockpit of the Natter would be too small to permit installation of an effective ejector seat. Furthermore, the use of such a seat would only serve to complicate a design intended to offer the very essence of simplicity. It was agreed therefore to dispense with the ramming attack; the pilot would jettison the forward fuselage complete with windscreen after discharging the rocket missiles, and this action would release the parachute-housing cover and deploy the chute. Detailed design progressed in parallel with wind tunnel trials at Braunschweig, and during tunnel testing speeds in excess of Mach 0.95 were simulated without the appearance of any adverse stability or compressibility effects.

The entire airframe of the Natter was of wooden construction, metal being used only for control push-rods, hinges and load-supporting attachment points. The fuselage was of semi-monocoque construction with laminated skin, stringers and formers, and the wing possessed a single laminated wooden spar which was continuous from wingtip to wingtip, and passed between the fuselage fuel tanks. The wing carried no movable surfaces, rolling control being obtained by differential operation of the elevons which formed part of the horizontal tail surfaces. The tail assembly might be described as of assymmetrical cruciform design in that the horizontal stabilizer was mounted above the fuselage and the vertical stabilizer extended below the fuselage. Large by comparison with the wing, the horizontal stabilizer contributed an important proportion of the total lift, both wing and stabilizer being of rectangular planform without dihedral, taper or sweep. The wing used a symmetrical aerofoil, with a thickness to chord of twelve per cent,and maximum thickness was located at fifty per cent chord.

Alternative forms of armament considered during the initial development stages included a cylindrical drum containing forty 30mm calibre shells fired by small rocket charges, and a battery of forty-nine similar missiles, but eventually a Bienenwabe (Honeycomb) arrangement of hexagonal tubes for 73mm Hs 217 Föhn (Storm) missiles or quadrangular tubes for R4M missiles was adopted, twenty-four of the larger or thirty-three of the smaller missile being decided upon after the test-firing of honeycomb containers accommodating varying quantities of missiles. Prior to the firing of the missiles, the forward end of the honeycomb container was to be enclosed by a jettisonable plastic cone.

As with the Heinkel and Junkers target-defence interceptors, considerable importance was attached to the provision of adequate armour protection for the pilot of the Natter, and the forward cockpit bulkhead was formed by an armour plate which was cut away at its base in order that the pilot's feet could reach the rudder pedals which were positioned one on each side of the missile honeycomb. Sandwich-type armour was provided on each side of the pilot's seat, and aft protection was afforded by a rear armour bulkhead which divided the cockpit from the fuel tanks. A simple ring sight was provided to assist the pilot in aiming the rocket missiles, and the fuel tanks were positioned immediately behind the cockpit rear bulkhead, the tank above the wing-spar containing 115 US gallons of T-Stoff and the tank below the spar accommodating fifty US gallons of C-Stoff.

In similar fashion to the Julia, the Natter was to be launched from a near-vertical ramp, the wingtips and

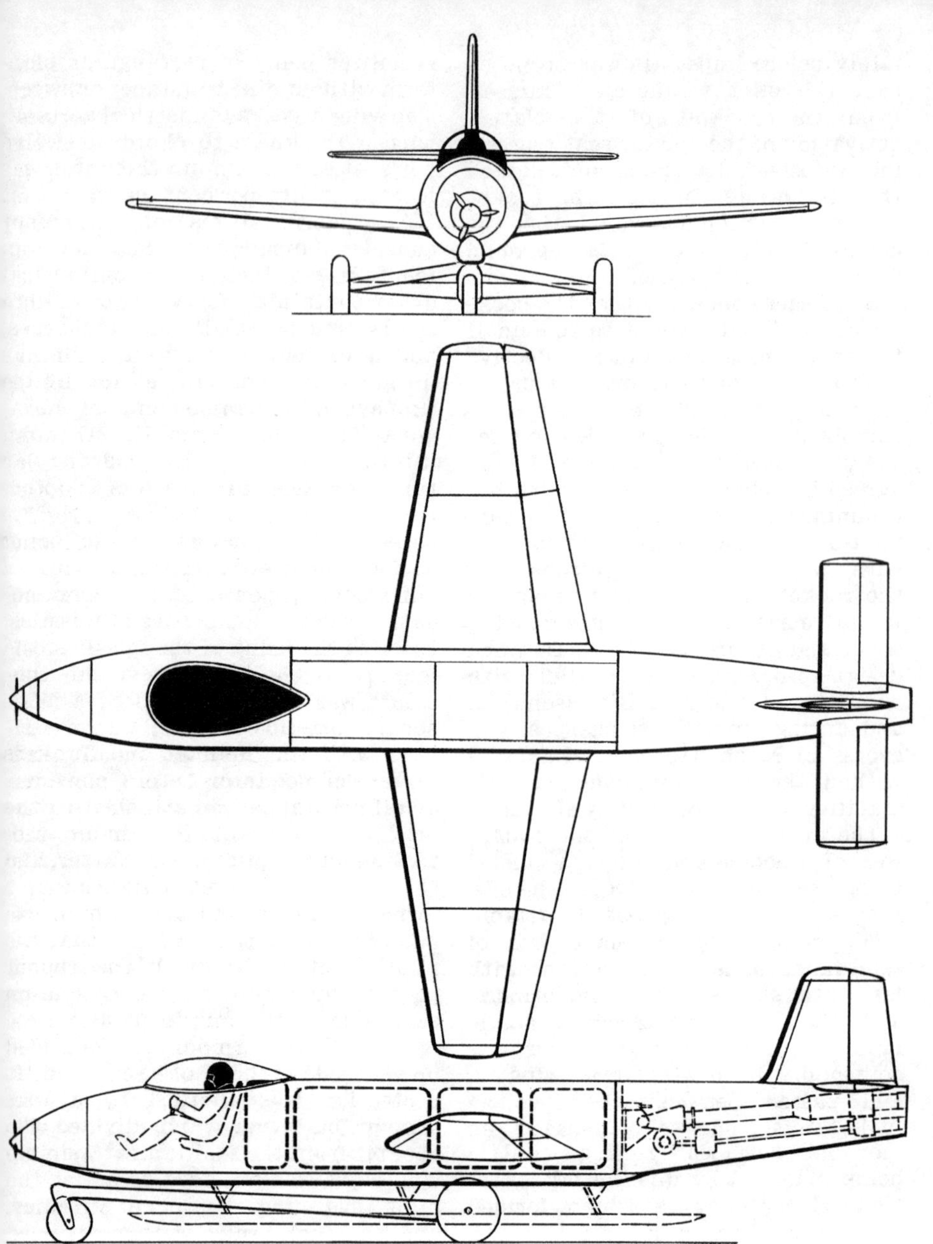

Runner-up to the Heinkel Julia was Junkers' EF 127, allocated the cover name of 'Dolly'. Offering better endurance than the Julia, Dolly was intended to take off with the aid of a three-wheel trolley and land on a long skid which was extended beneath the fuselage

the tip of the lower vertical stabilizer being strengthened to run in three guide rails. For take-off the thrust of the HWK 509A rocket motor (earlier plans to install the HWK 509C having been shelved) was to be supplemented by four 1,100-pound Schmidding booster rockets which it was expected would result in a 2.2 g vertical acceleration. A similar ground-controlled three-axis autopilot system to that proposed for the Julia was to operate after the burn-out of the boosters, and as the sole purpose of the Natter's pilot was to direct his airplane during the final phase of the attack on the enemy bomber formation, jettison the nose cone to expose the missiles, fire the entire complement of rockets in one salvo, turn away from the target and then bale out, the semi-expendable concept offered the possibility of employing personnel without any training other than that which could be provided on a rudimentary ground rig.

After completing his attack, the pilot was to release his seat harness, uncouple the control column, and release the safety catches and mechanical connections holding the nose section. This was then intended to separate from the remainder of the airplane, complete with windscreen, instrument panel, forward bulkhead and rudder pedals, simultaneously releasing a parachute housed in the rear fuselage. The sudden deceleration accompanying the deployment of this chute was expected to throw the pilot forward and clear of the airplane, and he would then descend in the normal fashion with his personal chute, the portion of the airframe containing the rocket motor being lowered to the ground for recovery.

Something of the impetus placed behind the Natter programme may be gauged from the fact that the first of an initial series of fifty test models of Bachem's radical warplane was completed at Waldsee within *three months* of the launching of the project. At this stage it was planned to use all fifty of these airplanes for gliding trials and for testing the Schmidding booster rockets, and the first of the pre-series Natters completed, which was referred to as the M 1, was tested in gliding flight in November 1944. Having no form of undercarriage, the Natter M 1 was mounted on a rudimentary three-wheeled trailer so that it could be towed into position for mounting beneath an Heinkel 111 bomber. Ballasted to a weight of 3,748 pounds, it was carried to an altitude of some 18,000 feet by the bomber and then released over the Heuberg Army Test Range. During this first flight, the pilot of the Natter dived the little airplane to attain a speed of 425mph, and after completing the scheduled test programme, baled out.

His subsequent report to the effect that the stability was excellent, and that the controls remained light and effective from 125mph up to the maximum speed attained, led to the idea of trying to land the unpowered Natter after each gliding test instead of abandoning the airplane. Therefore, the third airframe completed, Natter M 3, was fitted with a fixed tricycle undercarriage and a drogue chute which was to be deployed on touch-down anticipated to be in excess of 140mph. An attempt to land the Natter had still to be made when, on 18th December 1944, an empty airframe was fitted with the four Schmidding booster rockets, mounted on the launching ramp, and the rockets ignited. This test proved a complete failure, the Natter failing to leave the ramp owing to its rockets burning through the release cables.

A second attempt was made four days later, and on this occasion the Natter left the ramp as planned and disappeared into the cloud base at an altitude of 2,460ft. Ten more unmanned Natters were launched successfully, although it was ascertained that climbing speed by the time the booster rockets had burned out and were jettisoned (which was estimated to be closely comparable with that to

Above: **The first Bachem Natter prototype, the M 1, on the rudimentary trolley on which it was to be towed to the He 111 carrier. *Below:* The third Natter, the M 3, with its fixed tricycle undercarriage. *Right:* Pre-series Natters under construction at Waldsee**

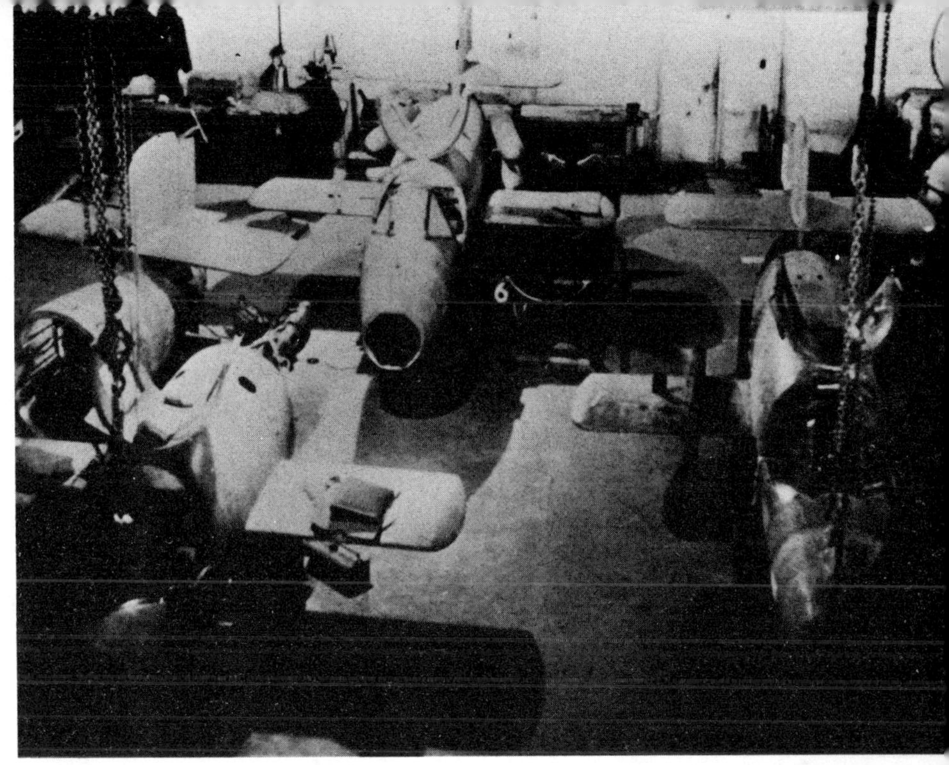

be attained by a fully tanked-up, manned Natter benefitting from the additional thrust of the HWK 509 rocket motor) was insufficient to result in full control surface effectiveness. To remedy this defect the vertical stabilizer was substantially enlarged, the upper rudder portion virtually doubled in chord, the ventral part of the fixed stabilizer being reduced in depth and elongated. The chord of the elevons was also increased, these changes being introduced on the Natter M 16 and all subsequent airplanes of this type built. At the same time it was proposed that small water-cooled control vanes be fitted in the rocket exhaust orifice of the powered model. It was calculated that these vanes would have a life only of some thirty seconds but that this would be long enough for sufficient speed to be attained to render the normal control surfaces fully effective.

By the time the first unmanned vertical launchings were attempted, something of the drive behind the Natter project had departed with Heinrich Himmler's loss of interest in the scheme. In fact, on 22nd December 1944, the day on which the first successful launching had been carried out, the meeting of the Chief Development Commission in Berlin, at which it was suggested that every means should be taken to expedite development of the Me 263, had decided that neither Heinkel's Julia nor Bachem's Natter held sufficient promise to warrant continued development and that the potential of the Me 263 and the turbojet-powered Me 262 fitted with supplementary rockets was such that these could well render all other target-defence interceptors superfluous. It was concluded, therefore, that work on the P 1077 Julia should be discontinued forthwith because of what was referred to as a 'totally inadequate' endurance; that work on Junkers EF 127 Dolly should be suspended, resumption of its development depending upon results achieved with the Me 263 and the rocket-boosted Me 262, and that development of the Natter, while opposed on both technical and tactical grounds, should be completed owing to the advanced stage that it had attained, but that all preparations for its series production should be discontinued at once.

The Commission's pronouncements were no more than reccomendations, and while they were acted upon in the case of the P 1077 Julia, work on which was abandoned and the prototype airframes scrapped, and the EF 127 Dolly, which was shelved, they were never implemented insofar as the Natter was concerned, although Bachem's interceptor was encountering problems unrelated to the disapproval of the pundits hundreds of miles away in Berlin. The behaviour of the Schmidding booster rockets was proving erratic, burning time and thrust varying, and several units exploding while under test at Waldsee. The Patin three-axis auto-pilot tended to be unreliable and difficult to synchronise, and promised deliveries of the HWK 509 had failed to materialise. In fact, the first Walter rocket motor was not to reach the Bachem-Werke until February 1945. On the other hand, the airframe had proved virtually trouble-free, demanding only 250 man-hours and being built for the most part by semi-skilled and unskilled labour, a number of small woodworking shops in and around the Black Forest producing laminated components.

It was not until 25th February that the first Natter to be fitted with the HWK 509A motor was ready for launching, and for the initial test a dummy was seated in the pilot's cockpit. The Natter left the launching ramp successfully and soared vertically into the sky, the booster rockets fell away on burn-out; at a predetermined altitude the nose section separated from the remainder of the airframe and both dummy pilot and power plant descended safely by parachute. By this time, with the skies over Germany rarely free of Allied aircraft, a sense of desperation reigned in the Air Ministry; a situation existed in which any straw was to be clutched at. The Air Ministry suddenly began to express interest in the Natter, and demanded that powered trials with a pilot aboard should commence immediately. Erich Bachem voiced his opinion that such tests were premature, and in this he was supported by Professor Ruff of the DVL, but all objections were dismissed out of hand, so that on 28th February, Oberleutnant Lothar Siebert, who had volunteered to test the Natter, climbed the near-vertical take-off ramp and clambered into a fully tanked-up airplane.

The folding hood was shut, the ground personnel climbed down the ramp, and Siebert set the control level of the HWK 509 motor in idling position. The onlookers waited anxiously while the turbine picked up speed. The Walter rocket ignited. Another pause while pressure built up in the combustion chamber, and then, with a tremendous roar, the four Schmidding booster rockets burst into life. A cloud of black smoke billowed around the base of the ramp and suddenly the Natter was climbing rapidly. The booster rockets fell away from the accelerating airplane and for a moment it seemed that all was well. Then the cockpit canopy flew off and the Natter flicked onto its back. Inverted, the airplane continued to climb, but at a shallower angle, reaching some 5,000ft before performing a half-loop, plummeting into the ground, and exploding on impact. Intensive investigation failed to produce an entirely satisfactory explanation for the accident, but it was assumed that the canopy may have been insecurely fastened prior to launching, and that Siebert had blacked-out.

Several pilots volunteered to take

A pre-series Natter airframe is prepared for a pilotless launching

Bachem Ba 349a Natter

1 Rudder
2 Rudder post/tailfin construction
3 Wooden tailfin construction
4 Wooden tailplane construction
5 Elevator
6 Exhaust orifice
7 Exhaust rudders
8 Control rod linkage
9 Jettisonable rocket clusters
10 Ventral rudder
11 Ventral fin
12 Launch rail strengthening
13 Combustion chamber
14 Rocket attachment eyes
15 Recovery parachute
16 Spring-operated container
17 Parachute exit hatch
18 Fore rocket attachment points
19 Fuselage break-point
20 Walter 509A rocket motor housing
21 T-Stoff tank
22 T-Stoff filler cap

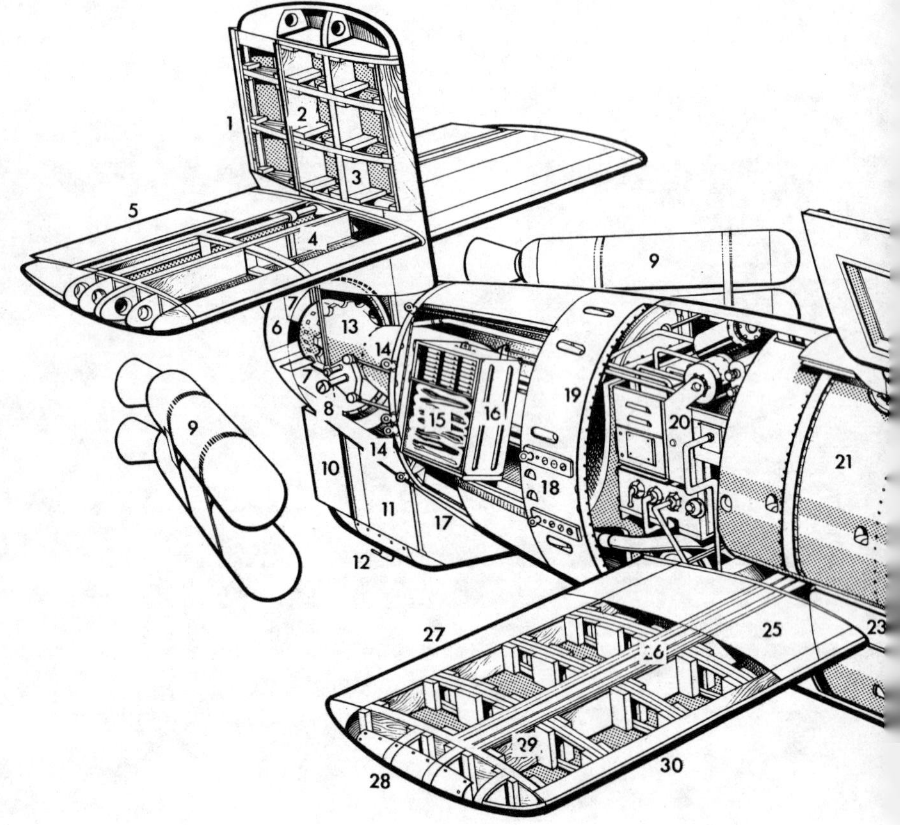

23 C-Stoff filler cap
24 C-Stoff tank
25 Wing skinning
26 Laminated mainspar (glued)
27 Solid rear spar/trailing edge
28 Wingtip launch rail strengthening
29 Wooden wing construction
30 Solid forward spar/leading edge
31 Hinged cockpit canopy
32 Side glazing
33 Roof glazing
34 Back armour
35 Head rest
36 Seat padding
37 Seat pan and harness
38 Control column
39 Instrument panel
40 Armoured windscreen
41 Recovery parachute cable
42 Rudder pedal
43 Instrument and rocket collector
44 Armoured bulkhead
45 Ring sight
46 Rocket tubes
47 24-s 217 'Föhn' rockets
48 Jettisonable plexiglas nose-cone

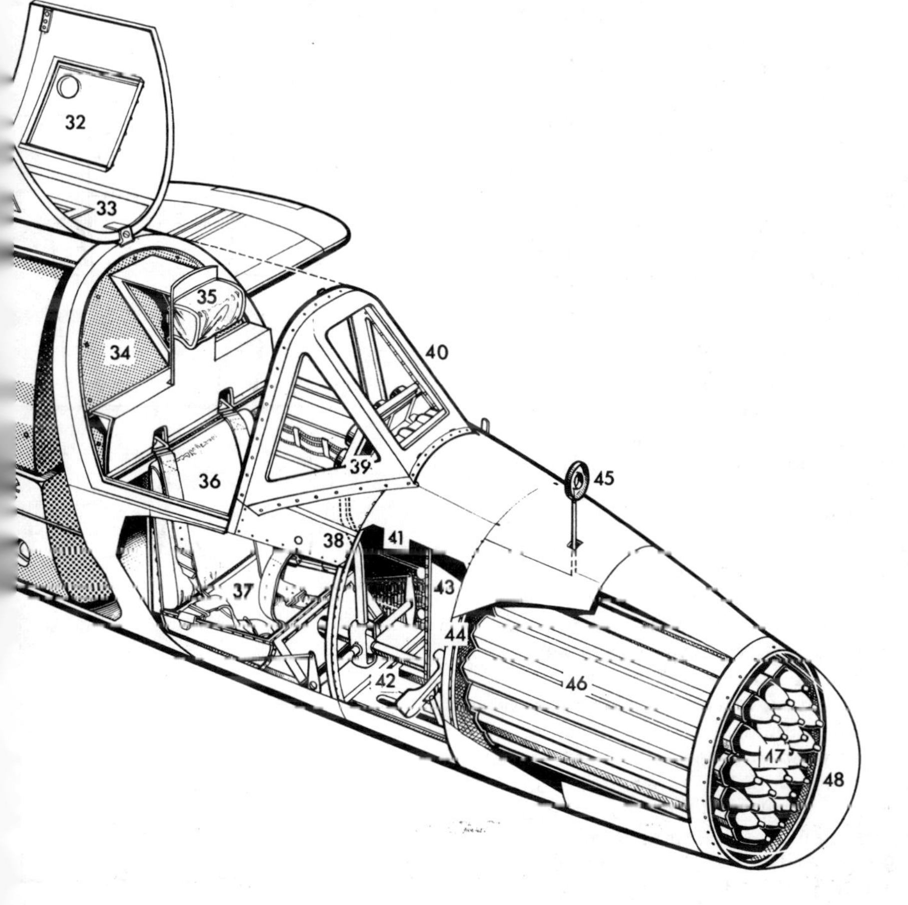

Siebert's place and the test programme continued. Three successful manned launchings were performed in rapid succession, and it was decided that the Natter had displayed an acceptable standard of reliability to warrant operational evaluation. Meanwhile, Bachem and Bethbeder, dissatisfied with the powered endurance of the Natter, had reverted to their original plan to use the HWK 509C motor with auxiliary cruising chamber. This dictated some redesign of the aft fuselage to accommodate the vertically-disposed rocket pipes and, for aerodynamic reasons, the lower contour of the fuselage was deepened marginally. No attempt was made to increase fuel capacity, but for CG reasons the attachment points for the booster rockets were moved aft, and provision was made to replace the four 1,100-pound rockets with two 2,205-pound Schmidding 533s.

These changes resulted in an increase in launching weight of only 127 pounds and flying weight was virtually unchanged, but powered endurance at 9,840ft and 495mph was increased from 2.23 to 4.36 minutes. It was de cided that the first-proposed proproduction model of the Natter should be discarded in favour of the modified BP 20B, as it was designated by the Bachem-Werke, or Ba 349B as it was known to the Air Ministry, and that the 51st Natter (ie, the first production airplane) would be completed to this standard. The BP 20B alias Ba 349B was expected to attain a top speed of 620mph at 16,400ft and an initial climb rate of 37,400ft per minute. Its range after climb was estimated at thirty-six miles at 19,685ft, and twenty-six miles at 29,530ft, and its take-off weight after the jettisoning of the booster rockets was 3,900 pounds.

It was probably the smallest interceptor ever built, spanning only 13ft 1½in from wingtip to wingtip, possessing a gross wing area of a mere 50.59 square feet, and measuring 19ft 9in from nose to tail, but the Natter

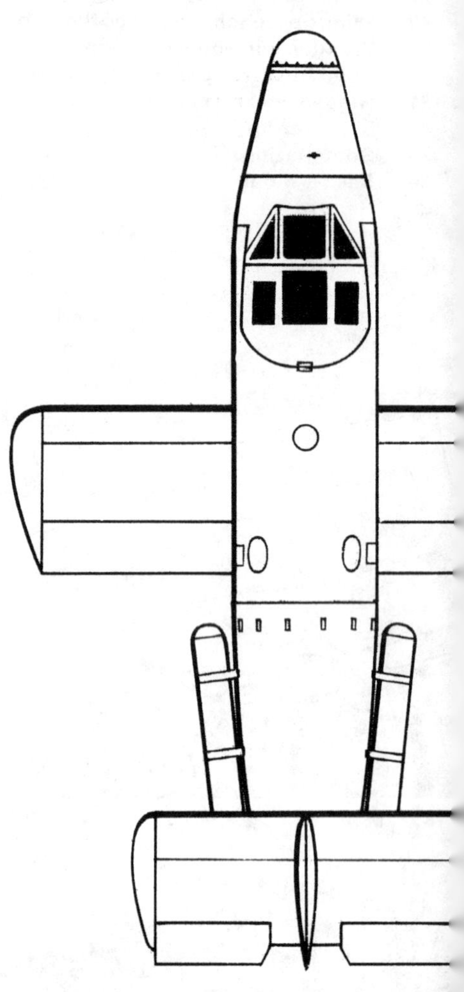

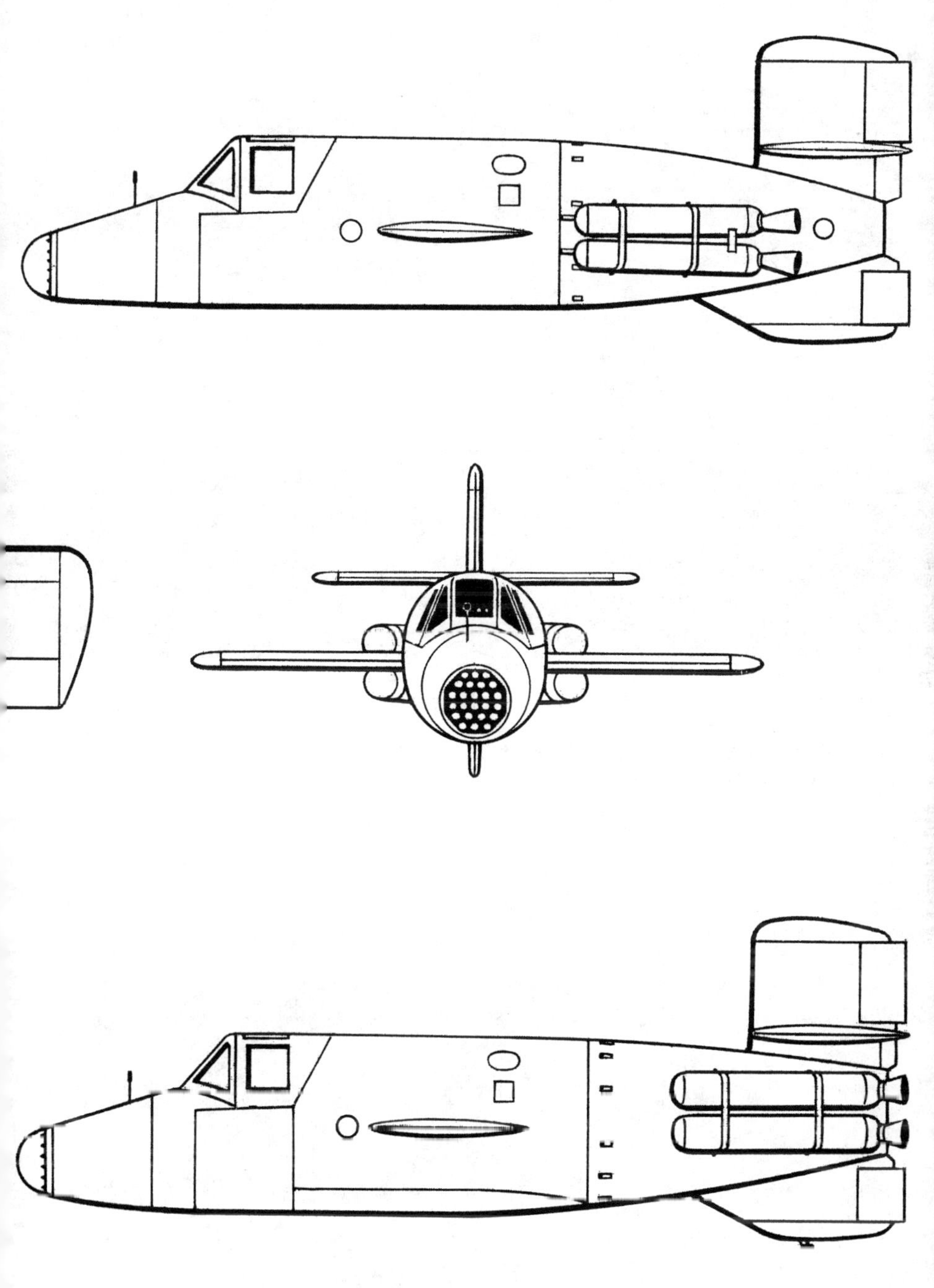

The plan, head-on, and upper sideview of the initial model of the Natter, the Ba 349A in its finalised form. The lower sideview shows the improved Ba 349B, the planned production model of this semi-expendable interceptor

Above: Siebert talking to Bachem immediately prior to the first and ill-fated pilot launching of the Natter. *Below:* Siebert is helped into the Natter cockpit on the take-off ramp. *Right:* The Natter, with Siebert aboard, immediately before the burn-out of the Schmidding boosters

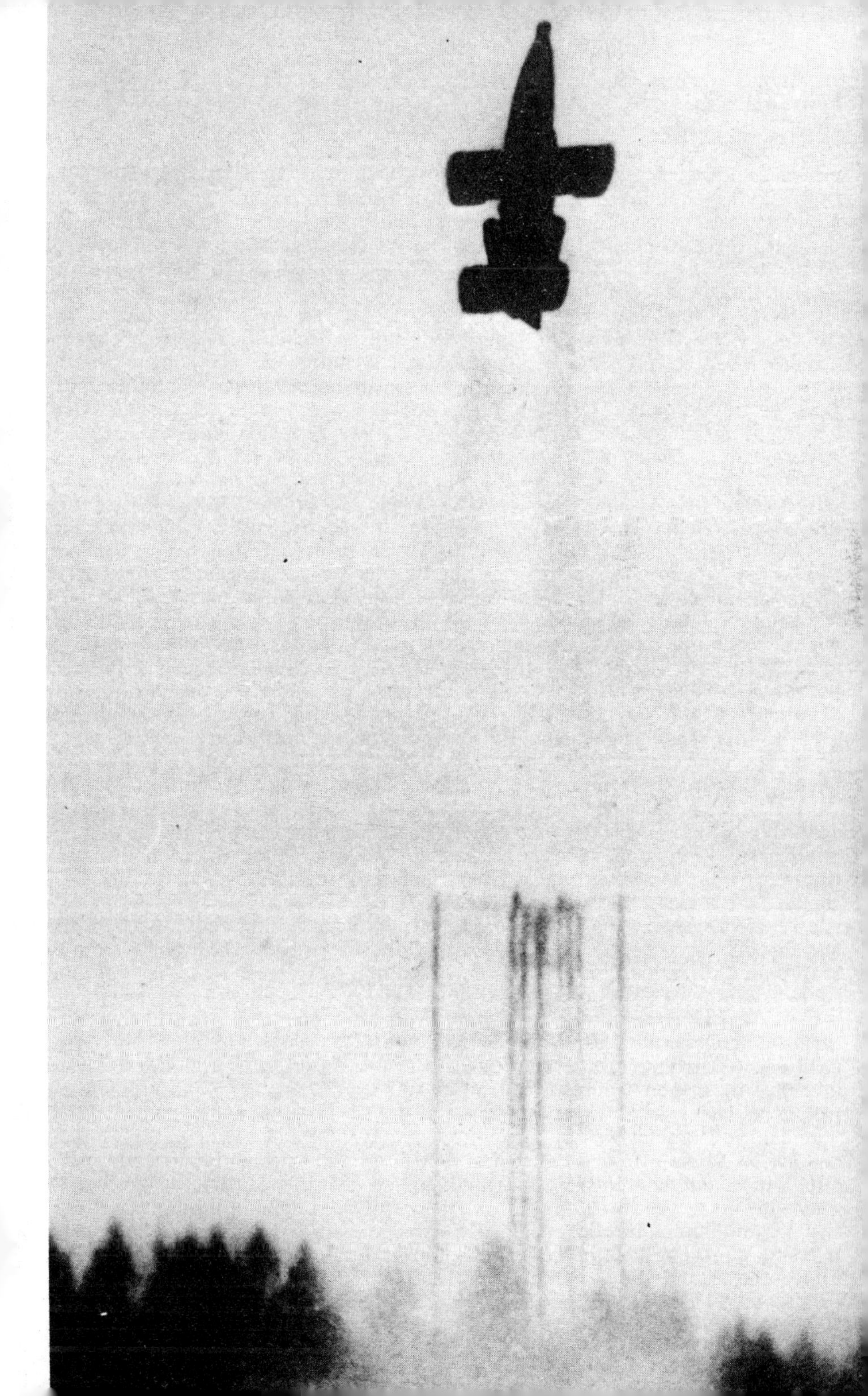

was to have no opportunity to demonstrate the potency of its sting. Operational evaluation was scheduled to commence in April 1945, and ten of the pre-series Natters were set up on ramps at Kirchheim, near Stuttgart, to await the arrival of an Allied bomber formation. In the event, Allied tanks reached the launching site before the expected bombers, and the Natters were destroyed on their ramps. At this time a total of thirty-six pre-series Natters had been completed at Waldsee, three of these to B-series standards, and of these three dozen experimental interceptors twenty-five had been flown either as gliders or in powered form, although only seven had been tested with pilots at the controls.

While the Natter was undoubtedly the most ingenious rocket-driven target-defence interceptor to fly, there were many equally ingenious designs which, while given serious consideration, failed to leave the drawing boards. One such was the Zeppelin 'Rammer' which, as its name suggested, was designed specifically to perform ramming attacks against enemy bombers, its immensely strong wing slicing through the target's tail assembly. Spanning 16ft 3in and having a length of 16ft 8¾in, the Rammer was to have had a very robust airframe making extensive use of steel. As originally proposed, the Rammer was to be fitted with a 2,205-pound Schmidding 533 solid-fuel rocket similar to the booster rockets intended to aid the take-off of other target-defence interceptors, and was to carry fourteen 55mm R4M rocket missiles in a honeycomb-type container in the nose. Weighing 1,896-pounds, the Rammer was to be towed or carried to an altitude above that of the approaching bomber formation, glide down to within 600 yards of a bomber and launch its rocket missiles in a single salvo. The pilot would then ignite the Schmidding rocket which would boost the speed of the Rammer to something of the order of 490mph, and aim the tiny airplane at the tail assembly of another bomber. If he survived the ramming attack, he would glide down, extend his landing skid and select a flat stretch of ground on which to alight.

The second-phase Rammer development envisaged the use of six powder rockets which were to be fired in sequence to boost speed to 530mph. With a somewhat greater all-up weight of 2,645-pounds, this version of the Rammer was to have had an even smaller wing, spanning only 14ft 9in, some twenty inches less than the span of another highly unorthodox target-defence interceptor project, the so-called 'midget' fighter proposed by Arado late in 1944. This tiny warplane, known to the Arado Flugzeugwerke by the project designation E 381, was intended to be suspended beneath an Arado 234C Blitz four-turbojet aircraft, featured a prone position for the pilot, and was to be powered by an HWK 509B rocket motor. The forward fuselage housing the prone pilot was to have been formed from a cylindrical tube of five millimetre armour which was claimed to provide complete protection from the 0.5in calibre weapons of the B-17 Fortresses, the pilot being provided a measure of visibility by a half-cone of Plexiglass enclosing a small armourglass screen.

The cylindrical armour tube also accommodated the two C-Stoff tanks which were situated on either side of the pilot's legs, and the T-Stoff container was immediately aft, separated from the pilot by a bulkhead. The HWK 509B was a simplified model of the basic rocket motor affording 880 pounds of thrust for an installed weight of 188 pounds, and proposed armament consisted of a single 30mm MK 108 cannon mounted in the stepped upper decking of the fuselage with forty-five rounds of ammunition carried in the port wing and aimed by means of a standard reflector sight. The single wing spar was to have been a thick-walled steel tube, and the skinning of the entire airplane was

The Me 163A tested by Adolf Niemeyer with R4M rocket missiles

envisaged as sheet steel. The overall length of the E 381 was 16ft 3in, and of the empty equipped weight of 1,962 pounds no less than 716 pounds represented the bare armoured nose section, all-up weight being 3,307 pounds.

The *modus operandi* called for the pilot of the 'midget' fighter to detach the intercom and heating circuit leads connecting the E 381 to the carrier aircraft, and release the suspension clips on sighting the intruding bomber formation. He would then glide towards the target, switch on the rocket motor and accelerate until he had attained a speed of some 125mph in excess of that of the formation of bombers, and open fire at point-blank range. It was calculated that the ammunition would suffice for two attacks on the bombers, and once this was expended the rocket motor was to be cut in order to leave a reserve of fuel for landing. The pilot would then glide down, using the rocket motor as necessary to find a suitable site on which to alight, and then extend the landing skid and deploy a 10ft braking chute. The Arado team was continuing development along the lines of the E 381 up to the time of Germany's surrender.

While design teams all over Germany were struggling to evolve really effective, rocket-propelled target-defence interceptors suitable for rapid mass production under the increasingly chaotic conditions existing in a beseiged Germany during the last months of fighting in Europe, the world's first rocket driven fighter unit, Jagdgeschwader 400, was exerting every effort to master the problems presented by the equipment that it did have, the Me 163B Komet. In September 1944, EK 16 had been transferred from Bad Zwischenahn to Brandis, some of the unit's personnel being sent to Udetfeld to form a training squadron initially known as the Ergänzungsstaffel (Replacement Squadron) of JG 400, this rapidly being

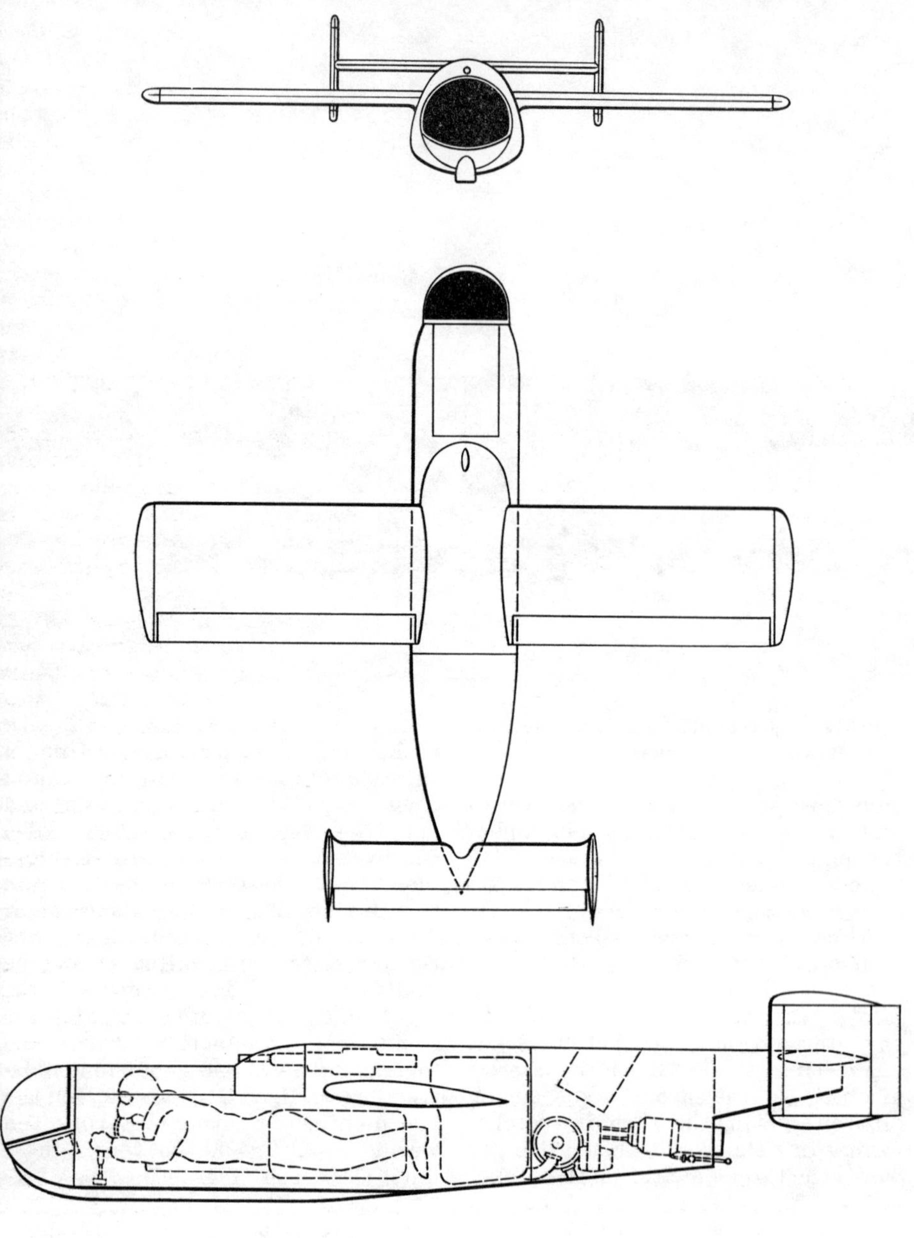

One of the most unconventional interceptor proposals was Arado's tiny E.381 project. This midget fighter was to have been carried aloft suspended beneath an Arado Ar 234 for launching as soon as the B-17 Fortresses appeared. Armament comprised a single 30mm cannon

expanded as 13 and 14 Staffeln of the III Gruppe of JG 400, and in December a II Gruppe consisting of 3 and 4 Staffeln had been formed at Stargard under the command of 'Pitz' Opitz, Major Wolfgang Späte having been recalled from the Eastern Front to take over as JG 400's Geschwaderkommodore from the first of that month. But time was now running out for JG 400 and the Komet.

Early combat experience and the poor results achieved with the MK 108 cannon had resulted in much thought being given to the possibility of alternative weapons for the Komet. When functioning efficiently the MK 108, which had been developed by Rheinmetall-Borsig and was being manufactured at a rate of 10,000 per month by the autumn of 1944, was a lethal weapon, one hit usually being sufficient to destroy a fighter and seriously damage a heavy bomber, but its range and rate of fire were insufficient for effective use at the closing speeds of the Komet and its target.

At Udetfeld an Erprobungskommando (Proving Detachment) shared the base with JG 400's III Gruppe, this special unit being engaged in experimentation with the R4M air-to-air rocket missile. Designed by Kurt Heber and developed and manufactured by the Deutsche Waffen-und-Munitionsfabrik at Lübeck, the R4M (Rakete – 4 kilos – Minen Geschoss, or 8.8-pound thin-walled rocket shell) was of 55mm calibre and contained 17.6 ounces of Hexogen which had a considerable blast effect. One of the III Gruppe instructors, Leutnant Adolf Niemeyer, conceived the idea of supplementing the Komet's MK 108 cannon armament with missiles of this type which had much the same trajectory as the 30mm gun and could therefore be used with the standard Revi 16B gun sight. He obtained the authorisation of the Geschwader Headquarters to perform trials with an Me 163A and fitted twelve R4M missiles beneath each wing. This external armament proved to have no adverse effect on the controllability of the airplane, and launched in a single salvo at the same distance from the target that a Komet pilot normally opened up with his cannon, they scattered to cover an area that would be occupied by a four-engined bomber. For several weeks Niemeyer performed tests which clearly indicated the possibilities of a Komet-R4M combination, but the scheme was discarded in favour of a somewhat more sophisticated and more spectacular armament.

Dr Langweiler, the inventor of the Panzerfaust (Tank Fist) one-man anti-tank weapon, proposed a revolutionary armament which, he claimed, would virtually guarantee a hit and probably a 'kill' by even the most inexperienced Komet pilot. This weapon, which was known as the SG 500 Jagdfaust (Fighter Fist), was simply a thin-cased 50mm high-explosive rocket-propelled shell housed in a vertical tube and fired by means of a photo-electric cell, or Foto-Zellenfühler, known as the Magische Aug (Magic Eye) and activated by the shadow of the target bomber. Five tubes were installed in each wing of a Komet, some thirty inches from the fuselage and splayed fanwise, and it was proposed that the Komet should fly beneath the bomber at maximum speed, the vertical separation being anything between sixty-five and 300 feet. Tests were conducted by flying the Komet beneath a canvas target suspended between two balloons, and successful results with these trials were followed by an actual test in combat, Leutnant Fritz Kelb operating the Jagdfaust against a B-17 which literally disintegrated. It was immediately decided to adopt this new armament as standard, but the modification of only twelve Komets was completed, and the modified interceptors were to be available too late to join combat.

The armament problems of JG 400 were compounded by training pro-

One of the pre-series Ba 349A Natters

blems as it became necessary to convert to the Komet pilots with only limited previous flying experience, and this led to the development of a tandem two-seat training glider, the Me 163S, which was a straightforward adaptation of the Me 163B airframe. The fuselage T-Stoff and ammunition tanks were removed from the bays immediately aft of the pilot's cockpit, and space was thus made available for a second cockpit with full dual controls, this being occupied by the instructor. Water ballast tanks were inserted in the fuselage on each side of the cockpit, and the wing C-Stoff tanks were also given over to water ballast, but the Me 163S was not destined to alleviate the training situation at Udetfeld as, before the first examples could be delivered, a Soviet armoured spearhead began to approach the base, necessitating the hurried evacuation of JG 400's III Gruppe. In January, it found itself at Brandis alongside the I Gruppe. Although by a strange quirk of fate the base at Brandis remained undamaged by bombing, the skies above were rarely free of Allied fighters and the risk of flying defenceless training gliders unacceptable.

From the beginning of 1945 the operational activities of JG 400 rapidly diminished. Komet activity was largely centered on Brandis where, by February when production of the Me 163B-1a finally terminated, more than a hundred brand new Komets were hidden beneath camouflage netting among the trees surrounding the field for want of pilots. There was also a critical shortage of rocket fuels which restricted the number of 'sharp starts'.

Some Komets of the I Gruppe were always at 'instant readiness', awaiting the order to take off on an intercept sortie, but such sorties had become extremely hazardous for there were invariably Allied fighters in the vicinity waiting for an opportunity to pounce on a helpless Komet which, having completed its mission and exhausted its fuel, was gliding in to land.

The last intercept sortie from Brandis was flown by Feldwebel Rolf Glogner, one of JG 400's most experienced Komet pilots, who took off shortly after dawn to intercept a reconnaissance Mosquito reported to be approaching Leipzig. Despite severe icing which seriously impaired vision from his cockpit, Glogner sighted the Mosquito below and some distance away, put the Komet into a steep dive and rapidly overhauled his quarry. Pulling out immediately behind the Mosquito, Glogner fired a short burst with his cannon and the port engine of the Mosquito immediately burst into flames, its two crew members baling out. The Komet had claimed another of the singularly few 'kills' to which it was to be able to lay claim during its brief operational career, but the life by now remaining to Germany's Third Reich could be counted in days.

The II Gruppe of JG 400 under 'Pitz' Opitz's command, which had been transferred from Stargard, near Neubrandenburg, to Husum, some twenty miles South of the Danish border, had achieved full operational strength, and only one thing prevented it participating in the final stages of the air war over Europe – fuel. The non-availability of supplies of rocket fuels kept II Gruppe's Komets grounded, and they sat out the last weeks of the war at Husum without once having flown in combat. Meanwhile, the remainder of the Jagdgeschwader had been breaking up, its most experienced pilots being hurriedly converted to the turbojet-driven Me 262, including its Kommodore, Wolfgang Späte, who, in March, had been posted to Jagdgeschwader 7. Insofar as JG 400 was concerned, it could claim only nine victims, discounting the immeasurably larger number of its own pilots claimed by the Komet in aborted take-offs, emergency landings, and in explosions while simply sitting on the runway. Neither was production of the Komet spectacular, a total of 237 being accepted by the Luftwaffe by the end of 1944, to these being added a further forty-two during the first two months of 1945 before production finally came to a halt as a result of the progressive disruption of communications and the failure of component supplies from the widely dispersed sub-contractors. Of these 279 production Me 163B-1a interceptors barely twenty-five per cent had actually been flown in combat.

Death of a concept

The closing phases of the Second World War had witnessed the beginning of the end of the pure rocket-driven interceptor, although this fact was apparent to few at the time, and a number of years were to elapse before the final burial. The mixed-power concept – turbojets being the primary source of power with a rocket motor available to boost take-off, climb, ceiling and speed as necessary – possessed obvious advantages from the operational viewpoint, although of necessity it demanded a more complex airplane, and did not readily lend itself to adaptation as a small, inexpensive and easily mass-produced warplane such as the German aircraft industry had tried to develop.

The mixed-power concept dated back to the mid 'thirties when the German air ministry first considered the rocket motor as a possible means of boosting for brief periods the performance of conventional pursuit airplanes. It had been in Germany too that the turbojet-cum-rocket fighter had been evolved during the final year of the war in the form of the Heimatschützer (Home Protector) version of Messerschmitt's Me 262. But the pure rocket-driven interceptor for point defence still had its adherents, despite the greater flexibility offered by mixed-power, and the Soviet Union, anxious to catch up with western technology, was intrigued by the wealth of data on rocket propulsion that its forces had found in Germany, attaching considerable importance to the development of a rocket-driven target-defence interceptor.

Power plant development in the Soviet Union in the immediate post-war years, as in other countries, placed emphasis on the turbojet, but Leonid Dushkin had continued experimental work on rocket motors after the termination of the rocket-driven interceptor programme in 1943, and, with the aid of data acquired from Germany, began the development of a new rocket motor in 1945 under the highest priority. This was intended for installation in a new target-defence interceptor, the task of designing which had been assigned the design bureau of Artem Mikoyan and Mikhail Gurevich.

In the meantime, several single- and two-seater Me 163 Komets had been taken to the Soviet Union for testing, but as it was found that powered trials would necessitate the opening of a special factory to produce hydrogen peroxide for the HWK 509 motor, the tests were confined to gliding trials in which several well known Soviet test pilots participated, including M Gallai, Ya I Vernikov, A A Efimov, and V A Golovastov. The Me 163, which received the appellation 'Karas' (Carp) from the Russian pilots, was usually towed into the air behind a Tupolev Tu-2 bomber, and was flown both with and without water ballast, dives up to the critical speed being made. The test pilots were highly critical of the landing skid arrangement, which resulted in more than one minor accident, and the consensus of opinion was that the unorthodox configuration of the Komet offered few advantages over more orthodox configurations and some serious disadvantages.

That this opinion was shared by Mikoyan and Gurevich was revealed in 1946 when this team's rocket-driven interceptor was rolled out and tested. Designated I-270 (Zh) – the suffix indicating Zhidkoye (toplivo), or Liquid (fuel) – the interceptor displayed clearly the debt that it owed the Junkers team at Dessau whose work had formed part of the booty acquired in the previous year by the Soviet Union. The fuselage was essentially that of the Ju 248 alias Me 263, and this had been married to a new, unswept laminar-profile wing and a slightly-swept horizontal stabilizer, the latter being mounted at the tip of the vertical surfaces. Although the undercarriage-well doors embodied some redesign, the tricycle undercarriage that they enclosed was virtually identical to that developed for the German fighter.

Proposed armament consisted of two 23mm NS-23 cannon, and the GRD-2M-3V (GRD = Gidroreaktivny dvigatel, or liquid reaction engine), using liquid oxygen and methanol-water, was of twin-chamber type, the main chamber providing a thrust of 3,200 pounds and the auxiliary cruising chamber furnishing 880 pounds. Possessing a wing area of 129.17 square foot, which was substantially less than that of its German forerunner, this Germano-Russian *mélange* had an empty equipped weight of 4,409 pounds and a normal loaded weight of 9,039 pounds, the latter providing what was, for 1946, the somewhat daunting wing loading at take-off of seventy pounds per square foot. However, the requirement to which the I-270 (Zh) had been designed had placed emphasis on climbing capability, manoeuvrability being a very secondary consideration, and this small target-defence interceptor could reach 32,800 feet in 2.37 minutes and 49,200 feet in 3.03 minutes. Maximum level speed was 620mph, full-thrust endurance was four-and-a-quarter minutes while powered endurance on the auxiliary cruising chamber only after climbing to 32,800 feet was nine-and-a-quarter minutes. But Mikoyan and Gurevich's contribution to the story of the rocket-driven target-defence interceptor was destined to be the swansong of this class of aircraft in the Soviet Union. The requirement to which the I-270 (Zh) had been designed had been overtaken by a new specification before it had even flown.

Early in 1946, Soviet research institutes, having worked overtime in their attempt to absorb the deluge of German theoretical and research data on wing sweepback, had concluded that an infinitely more flexible interceptor powered by a turbojet and offering a performance superior in all respects other than climb rate to that of a rocket-driven airplane could be evolved by sweeping the wing. Accordingly, the Soviet Air Forces had drafted a specification for such an interceptor, and to this Mikoyan and Gurevich's design bureau had commenced work on what was then known as the I-310 in March 1946, several months before the I-270 (Zh) began its flight test programme; work which was to have a profound effect on western design thinking when, three years later, it was to be revealed to the world as the MiG-15.

After the abortive attempt to produce the Northrop XP-79 rocket-driven interceptor, the USA had lost interest in the rocket as a prime mover for manned combat aircraft, confining this form of propulsion to high-speed research vehicles, although during the late 'forties the USAF was to have a fleeting honeymoon with the mixed-power concept in the unique shape of the Republic XF-91 which coupled a General Electric J47 turbojet with a Reaction Motors XLR11-RM-9 rocket motor running on liquid oxygen and ethyl alcohol in an attempt to combine the point intercept and area intercept tasks in one airplane. It was Britain, a late starter in the field of rocket propulsion, that was to write *finis* to the story of the rocket-driven target-defence interceptor.

The development of liquid-propellant rocket motors in Britain did not really get into its stride until after the war, when, in 1946, Armstrong Siddeley Motors received a contract to develop a rocket of 2,000-pounds thrust for use by interceptors designed to the mixed-power formula. Simultaneously, the de Havilland Engine Company embarked upon rocket motor development and received a Ministry of Supply contract to continue this work in 1947. Hawker Aircraft had been among the first British aircraft manufacturers to see the potentialities of the turbojet-cum-rocket arrangement for point and area interceptors and shipboard fighters, and as early as October 1945 had made proposals for such combat airplanes.

At that time, Hawker Aircraft was preparing to commence construction of prototypes of its P.1040, an aesthetically superb design that was to emerge as the Sea Hawk shipboard fighter, and had proposed two mixed-power derivatives, the P.1046 and P.1047 with unswept and swept wings respectively. Both studies envisaged a rocket motor in the extreme rear fuselage, but as no such power plant had then existed in Britain there had been little point in pursuing their development. Armstrong Siddeley's contract for a 2,000-pound thrust rocket motor led, in 1946, to a series of Hawker schemes for mixed-power fighters under the generic project designation P.1053, and in the follow-

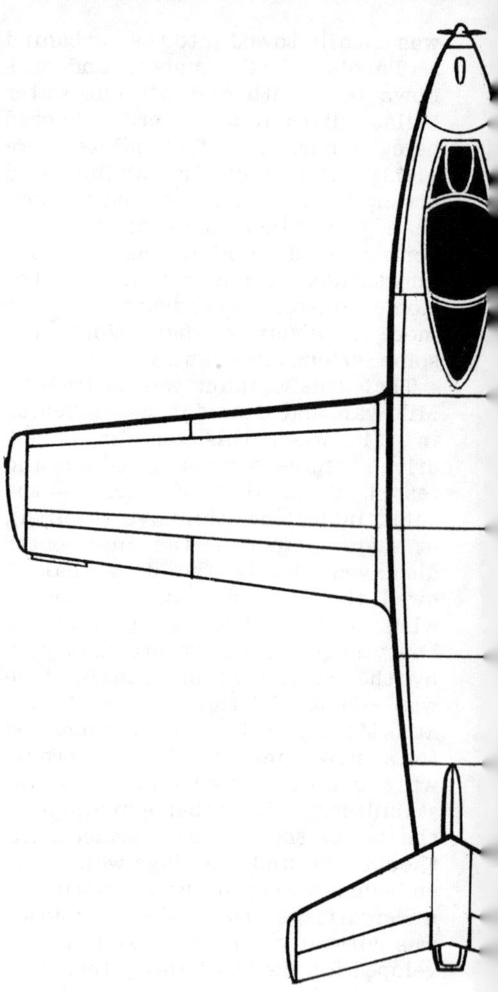

The last rocket-driven target-defence interceptor to be built and flown, the I-270 (Zh). It was evolved by Mikoyan and Gurevich, who drew heavily on material captured by Soviet forces with the occupation of the Junkers plant at Dessau. Its relationship to the Me 263 is obvious

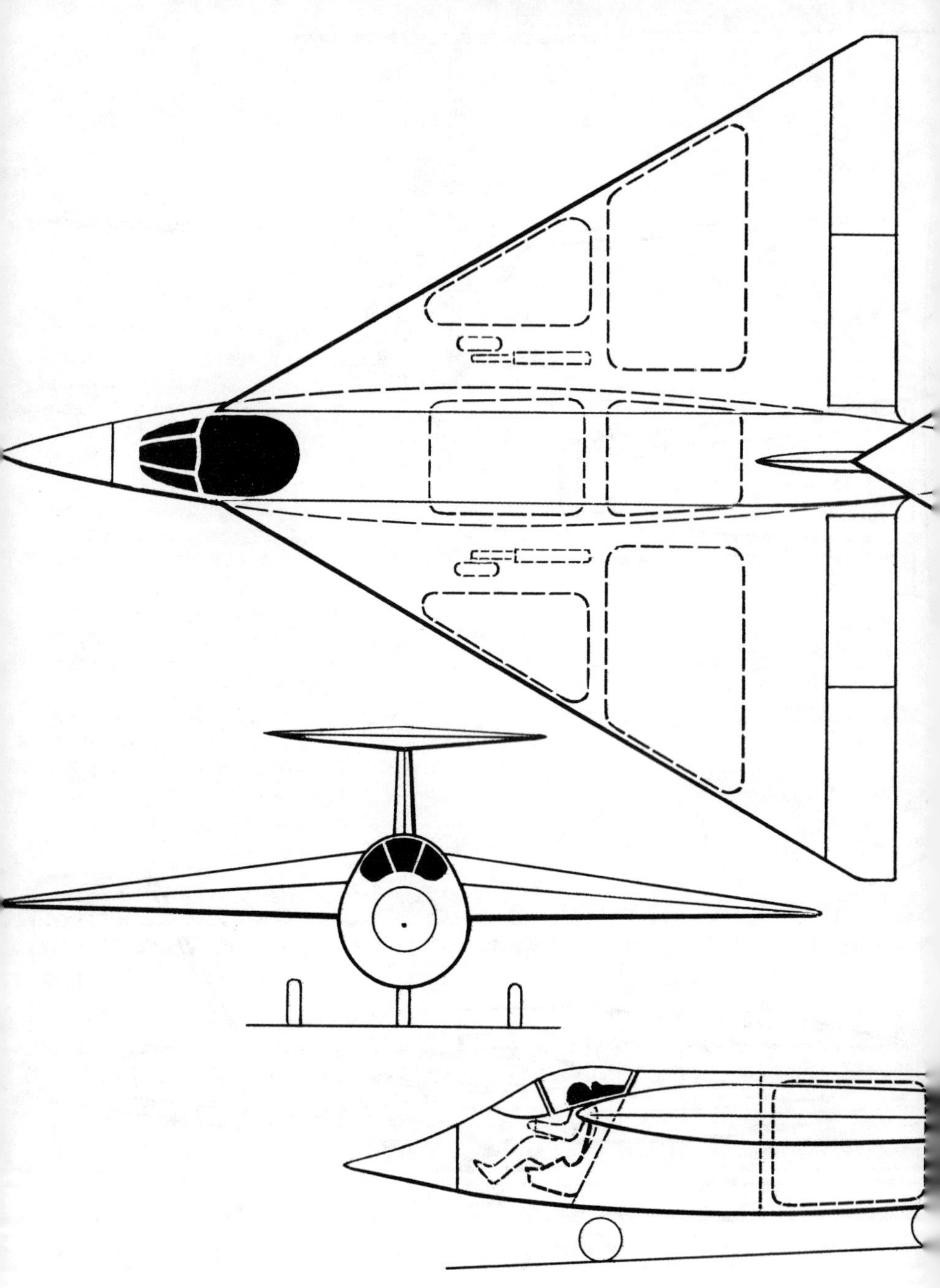

The Short P.D.7 project, one of several proposals tendered to meet the requirements of Specification F.124 which called for a pure rocket-propelled interceptor. This requirement was eventually abandoned in favour of F.137 and F.138 which called for a mixed-power fighter

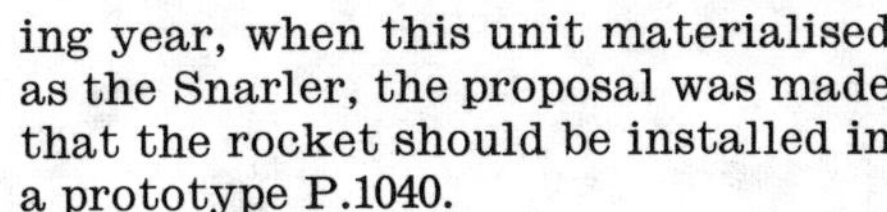

ing year, when this unit materialised as the Snarler, the proposal was made that the rocket should be installed in a prototype P.1040.

The Snarler used methanol-water as fuel and liquid oxygen as an oxidant, weighed 215 pounds and could be run for an indefinite period. Work on converting the P.1040 to take this rocket motor began in September 1949, a 144 US gallon methanol-water tank was introduced, together with a 90 US gallon liquid oxygen container, and the Snarler was fitted in the extreme tail. On 20th November 1950 the rocket was ignited for the first time, and, as the P.1072, the aircraft flew a half-dozen times, a minor explosion causing some damage during the last of these flights. A 1949 proposal to undertake a similar conversion of the swept-wing P.1052 design as the P.1078 progressed no further than the study stage as operational requirements were changing. The threat of the high-altitude bomber flying at high subsonic speeds and carrying a nuclear load now dominated all defence thinking, and as one potential antidote, Britain, somewhat surprisingly, reverted to the pure rocket-driven target-defence interceptor.

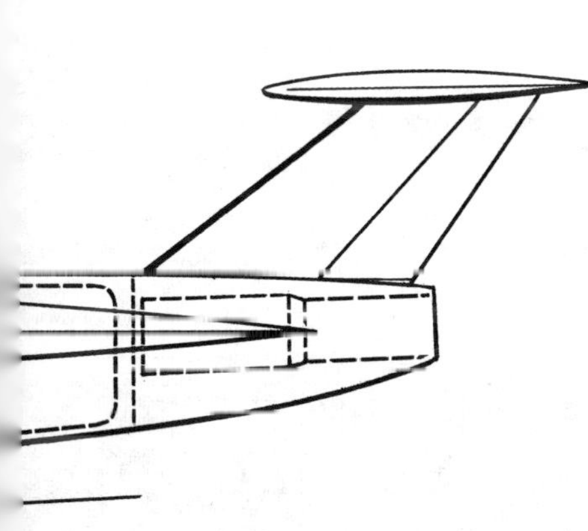

While de Havilland Engine Company had been developing a cold type rocket motor of 5,000 pounds thrust primarily for assisting the take-off performance of heavily-laden aircraft, this monopropellant power plant known as the Sprite using HTP (high-test peroxide) and providing sixteen seconds of full thrust, Armstrong Siddeley had been engaged on the design of a new rocket based on the company's experience with the Snarler. This new power plant was intended from the outset to propel a supersonic interceptor and was dubbed the Screamer. As originally conceived in 1950, the Screamer was to have afforded 4,000 pounds of thrust and, like its predecessor, use methanol-water and liquid oxygen, but when the Ministry of Supply in-

VP401
VP401

Above left: **The first flight under rocket power in Britain was performed by the Hawker P.1072.** ***Left:*** **The Snarler rocket motor in the tail of the Hawker P.1072 fighter** ***Above:*** **The Mikoyan-Gurevich I-270 (Zh) reveals its German ancestry in the contours of the fuselage**

vited tenders for a pure rocket-propelled high-altitude interceptor to specification F.124, the thrust requirement increased considerably, and a change from methanol to kerosene or wide-cut gasoline was specified. It was also decided to feed water into the combustion chamber for cooling purposes, and an 8,000-pound thrust was demanded.

Specification F.124 produced several tenders, including the Bristol 178, the Hawker P.1089, the Short P.D.7, and the Saunders-Roe S-R.53, and envisaged a performance markedly in advance of any rocket-driven interceptor previously conceived, calling for a design theoretically capable of speeds of the order of Mach 2.0 at a time when no fighter extant had surpassed Mach 1.0 in level flight. But advanced though the speed performance demanded by the specification may have been, F.124 still suffered all the principal shortcomings of earlier pure rocket-driven interceptors. Essentially a short-range airplane, it has to be launched from bases almost in the line of approach of intruding bombers, these bases having to be around the coastline or as close as possible to the bombers' probable targets. In either case, a large number of bases were necessary.

This posed the problem of getting the rocket-driven interceptors to the appropriate bases. Ferrying by air presented obvious difficulties, and transportation by road was undesirable as such would necessitate detachable wings with a consequent penalty in structural weight. If transported in one piece the aircraft would block the roads and interfere with other military traffic. Although the interceptor was intended to achieve

The Saunders-Roe S-R.53 cruises on the power of its turbojet

Mach 2.0, at that point in time it was not known if combat at such speeds was practical and, in any case, the substantial quantities of fuel necessary for acceleration rendered their attainment improbable.

Typical of the proposals tendered to meet F.124 was the Short P.D.7 which embodied a sixty-degree delta planform which facilitated the stowage of the large volume of fuel demanded by the specification. The delta wing spanned thirty feet and had a gross area of 420.3 square feet and a constant thickness/chord ratio of nine per cent, this housing four tanks containing 3,208 pounds of kerosene, and the main members of the tricycle undercarriage. The fuselage, which had an overall length of 35ft (this being increased to 39ft 9in by the swept vertical stabilizer), accommodated the pilot, armament, two tanks containing 8,012 pounds of liquid oxygen, and the Screamer rocket motor. The all-up weight at take-off was calculated at 19,935 pounds and empty equipped weight being 7,910 pounds.

It was estimated that the P.D.7 would take just short of a minute to accelerate to climbing speed from a standing start and would use 2,175 pounds of fuel. An altitude of 30,000 feet would be attained in 2.87 minutes for the consumption of a further 4,545 pounds of fuel, and 60,000 feet in 3.72 minutes, by which time a total of 8,700 pounds of fuel would have been consumed. This would leave sufficient fuel for ten minutes subsonic patrol and two minutes of combat at Mach 0.95, with virtually no allowance for landing. Elementary calculations revealed the impracticability of this concept. Assuming the intruding bomber to be travelling at Mach 0.9 at 60,000 feet, the P.D.7 reaching the apex of its climb to the same altitude at Mach 0.9 and then accelerating to pursue its target would gain only ten

suming miles on the bomber before c ccessful its last fuel, its chances of a s interception being negligibl ns had

Much the same conclus mpanies been reached by all the c or pre- that had submitted tender he pure pared outline proposals. The inter- rocket-propelled target-defen propo- ceptor was no longer a viab his fact, sition. Finally convinced of uirement the Ministry amended its req ng speci- to include a turbojet, issu e former fications F.137 and F.138, t 720 which being met by the Avro with an coupled a Screamer rocket turbojet, Armstrong Siddeley Viper lled by a and the latter being fulfil .53 which reworked Saunders-Roe S-R petitor of coupled de Havilland's com arly-rated the Screamer, the simil with HTP Spectre using kerosene . Thus, as as an oxidant, with a Viper ath knell the 'fifties dawned the dea ed inter- for the pure rocket-propell ot that ceptor was finally rung. N fighters either of the mixed-power from that had indirectly stemmed F.124 were long to survive the demise of the pure rocket fighter, the Avro 720 being scrapped before completion in the economy drive held in Britain in 1956, and the S-R.53, although flown in prototype form, being over- taken by a more advanced design to the same mixed-power formula, the S-R.177, this in turn becoming a casualty of Britain's infamous 1957 White Paper on Defence which (tem- porarily as events were to prove) terminated the further development of manned fighters.

The rocket-driven target-defence interceptor concept, born in the late 'thirties, had died at the beginning of the 'fifties, at a time when rocket technology had finally advanced suf- ficiently to render the airplanes to which it had given life a somewhat less frightening prospect from the pilot's viewpoint. Its life span had measured barely more than a decade; its gest- ation had been protracted, its infancy prolonged, and it had never seen maturity.

Bibliography

The Luftwaffe War Diaries by Cajus, Bekker (Macdo
German Secret Weapons by Brian J Ford (Ballantinald, London)
The First and the Last by A Galland (Methuen, LondNew York)
Warplanes of the Third Reich by William Green (Maon)
The Luftwaffe, A History by Jorn Killen (Muller, Ldonald, London)
German Secret Weapons of the Second World War by ndon)
Die Deutschen Flugzeuge 1933–1945 by Heinz NowarR Lusar (Spearman, London)
Luftwaffe by Alfred Price (Ballantine, New York) a (Lehmanns, Munich)
German Research in World Warr II by L E Simon (W
Rockeet Fighter by Mano Ziegler (Macdonald, Londiley, New York)
on)

William Green

Rocket Fighter

Rocket Fighter